Fate the Hunter

Library of Arabic Literature

General Editor
Philip F. Kennedy, New York University

Executive Editors
James E. Montgomery, University of Cambridge
Shawkat M. Toorawa, Yale University

Editorial Director
Chip Rossetti

Assistant Editor
Leah Baxter

Editors
Sean Anthony, The Ohio State University
Huda Fakhreddine, University of Pennsylvania
Lara Harb, Princeton University
Maya Kesrouany, New York University Abu Dhabi
Enass Khansa, American University of Beirut
Bilal Orfali, American University of Beirut
Maurice Pomerantz, New York University Abu Dhabi
Mohammed Rustom, Carleton University

Consulting Editors
Julia Bray • Michael Cooperson • Joseph E. Lowry
Tahera Qutbuddin • Devin J. Stewart

Digital Production Manager
Stuart Brown

Paperback Designer
Nicole Hayward

Fellowship Program Coordinator
Amani Al-Zoubi

Letter from the General Editor

The Library of Arabic Literature makes available Arabic editions and English translations of significant works of Arabic literature, with an emphasis on the seventh to nineteenth centuries. The Library of Arabic Literature thus includes texts from the pre-Islamic era to the cusp of the modern period, and encompasses a wide range of genres, including poetry, poetics, fiction, religion, philosophy, law, science, travel writing, history, and historiography.

Books in the series are edited and translated by internationally recognized scholars. They are published in parallel-text and English-only editions in both print and electronic formats. PDFs of Arabic editions are available for free download. The Library of Arabic Literature also publishes distinct scholarly editions with critical apparatus.

The Library encourages scholars to produce authoritative Arabic editions, accompanied by modern, lucid English translations, with the ultimate goal of introducing Arabic's rich literary heritage to a general audience of readers as well as to scholars and students.

The publications of the Library of Arabic Literature are generously supported by Tamkeen under the NYU Abu Dhabi Research Institute Award G1003 and are published by NYU Press.

Philip F. Kennedy
General Editor, Library of Arabic Literature

About this Paperback

This paperback edition differs in a few respects from its dual-language hardcover predecessor. Because of the compact trim size the pagination has changed. Material that referred to the Arabic edition has been updated to reflect the English-only format, and other material has been corrected and updated where appropriate. For information about the Arabic edition on which this English translation is based and about how the LAL Arabic text was established, readers are referred to the hardcover.

Fate the Hunter

Early Arabic Hunting Poems

TRANSLATED BY
James E. Montgomery

FOREWORD BY
Alice Oswald

VOLUME EDITOR
Richard Sieburth

NEW YORK UNIVERSITY PRESS
New York

NEW YORK UNIVERSITY PRESS
New York

Please contact the Library of Congress for Cataloging-in-Publication data.

ISBN: 9781479834259 (paperback)
ISBN: 9781479834273 (library ebook)
ISBN: 9781479834266 (consumer ebook)

This book is printed on acid-free paper, and its binding materials are chosen for strength and durability. We strive to use environmentally responsible suppliers and materials to the greatest extent possible in publishing our books.

Series design and composition by Nicole Hayward.

Typeset in Adobe Text

Manufactured in the United States of America

10 9 8 7 6 5 4 3 2 1

To the memory of my parents,
Arthur John and Elizabeth Montgomery (née Conner),
who kitted me out and set me on my way.

Contents

Letter from the General Editor / iii
Acknowledgments / xiii
Foreword / xv
Introduction / xxiii
Map: The Tribes of Pre-Islamic Arabia / xxxvii
Note on the Text / xxxix
Notes to the Introduction / xliii

Fate the Hunter / 1

1 Imru' al-Qays: Echoes of Love Lost / 3
2 'Abīd ibn al-Abraṣ: That Mighty Hunter the Eagle / 8
3 'Abīd ibn al-Abraṣ: The Seas of Poetry / 12
4 Al-Muraqqish al-Akbar: When Vultures Enter the Tents / 14
5 Al-Shanfarā: Like a Spleen-Dark Wolf / 17
6 Ṣakhr al-Ghayy: The Workings of Fate / 21
7 Labīd ibn Rabī'ah: In the Grip of the North Wind / 23
8 Al-Muzarrid ibn Ḍirār: My Flood of Words / 29
9 Abū Dhu'ayb: Fate the Hunter / 34
10 Al-Ḥuṭay'ah: Slaughter Me, Father / 38
11 Ḥumayd al-Arqaṭ: A Tall-Necked Horse / 40
12 Ghaylān ibn Ḥurayth: A Hunter since Her Youth / 41
13 Ghaylān ibn Ḥurayth: A Stipple-Cheeked Gos / 42
14 Al-Shamardal ibn Sharīk: Her Assegai Beak / 43
15 Al-Shamardal ibn Sharīk: His Dark Elation / 45
16 Al-Shamardal ibn Sharīk: An Irate Stare / 46

17 Al-Shamardal ibn Sharīk: A Dark Gos / 48
18 Al-Shamardal ibn Sharīk: Like a Mill / 49
19 Al-Shamardal ibn Sharīk: Clothes Ignite / 50
20 Al-Shamardal ibn Sharīk: Like Two Rubies / 51
21 Al-Shamardal ibn Sharīk: Dawn Shines Pink / 52
22 Abū l-Najm al-ʿIjlī: Harried by the Jinn / 53
23 Abū l-Najm al-ʿIjlī: Dyed Dark with Gore / 57
24 Abū l-Najm al-ʿIjlī: Full of Bloodlust / 63
25 Abū l-Najm al-ʿIjlī: Coils Scraping on Coils / 65
26 Abū l-Najm al-ʿIjlī: The Hills Shimmered / 70
27 ʿAbd al-Ḥamīd al-Kātib: To the Beat of the Drums / 74

Note to the English Translation / 79
Glossary / 109
Bibliography / 119
Further Reading / 125
Index / 127
About the NYUAD Research Institute / 139
About the Translator / 140
The Library of Arabic Literature / 141

In a way, I suppose, I think of poems as a sort of animal. They have their own life, like animals, by which I mean they seem quite separate from any person, even from their author, and nothing can be added to them or taken away without maiming and perhaps even killing them.

TED HUGHES, *POETRY IN THE MAKING.*

He is over them and behind, rowing hard, very fast,
somewhere a heron alarms, and jackdaws' cackling chorus
I don't see the snatch, but the heavier goshawk is past
and the present is that bewilderment—not nothing for us
for we have been hunters, and, some of us, slightly aware
or intensely engaged at the fringe of emotion, scare
the goshawk is big enough to deliver, and, so, rare.

COLIN SIMMS, "PM, 6 JAN 2016 BY THE RIVER IRTHING," *GOSHAWK POEMS.*

Acknowledgments

This project has kept me company for three and a half decades. I have amassed more debts of gratitude in the intervening years than I can recall, and am profoundly grateful to all those who have helped me at any time and in any way with this material.

This book began life a decade ago. I doubt I would ever have visited the Abu Dhabi Falcon Hospital were it not for my involvement with the Library of Arabic Literature. Since LAL's inception in 2010, I have learned much about Arabic, Arabic literature, and English from my colleagues on the editorial board, and have come to appreciate why the humanities are so called. LAL's visits to NYU Abu Dhabi owe most of their success to the wonderful staff of the NYU Abu Dhabi Institute. Gila Waels, Manal Demaghlatrous, Nora Yousif, Antoine El Khayat, and Amani Al-Zoubi have been with us every step of the way. Thank you all!

My edition and translation of ʿAbd al-Ḥamīd's *risālah* benefited greatly from the generosity and erudition of professors Bilal Orfali and Anna Akasoy. It is thanks to them that I decided to include it in this book. Professor Clive Holes helped me understand Shaykh Zayed's poem and provided crucial information on the flora of the region. Helen Macdonald accepted my invitation to lunch and looked at a couple of my early translations. Sir Mark Allen KCMG kindly gave me lunch, commented on drafts of some Abū Nuwās poems, offered kümmel, and loaned me a book. Amira Bennison supported my application for leave. The Department of Middle Eastern Studies and Trinity Hall, my institutional homes at Cambridge, have always been supportive. And my Cambridge colleague Charis Olszok's invitation to lecture at her conference in December 2021 forced me to make my mind up about the final shape of the book and the project. Her expertise in critical animal studies and ecocriticism has encouraged me to up my game.

My friends on LAL's executive board have been paragons of forbearance and encouragement as I worked to bring coherence and shape to my project. It is thanks to the friendship and perseverance of Phil Kennedy, Shawkat Toowara, Chip Rossetti, and Lucie Taylor that this book has seen the light of day. And thank you, Stuart Brown, Keith Miller, and Wiam El-Tamami—as always, you have produced such a handsome book.

Involvement in LAL has brought many good things into my life. Principal among them is my friendship with Richard Sieburth, my volume editor. Richard took a project that was stuck in the doldrums and filled its sails. Our work together on these poems has been a delight. I may not always have followed his advice, but it was never lightly ignored. I am already looking forward to our next round of creative engagement.

Readers who know me personally will know that the last ten years have not been kind to my family. If I'm pinching myself that I've reached the stage of writing a page of acknowledgments, it is a testimony to their belief in me. Yvonne, Natasha, Sam, and Josh, with the help of Reggie, our Jack Russell terrier, help me make sense of it all.

Foreword

ALICE OSWALD

In midwinter, *Fate the Hunter* arrives at my door. It is raining and I'm glad to bring this desert voice into the room. The skylight is blurred, the city is misted, but up here in the top of the house there is a world inside the world and it is very light and the poems seem to blow through me leaving a layer of sand.

When I put the book down, before reading footnotes or introduction, I have an impression of whirling speed. Similes flash past: an ostrich like a bucket dropping down a well, a horse like a lunatic undressing, wounds like rips in cloth, teats like earrings, legs like striped cloaks, wolves like the clack of arrows. My senses move more quickly than my thoughts, as if I had been reading while running.

Every poem is flying fast and hitting something. Thwack, thud, crack: these are the sounds used by James Montgomery to translate the moment when a missile kills an animal. The impact makes a vortex in the language, the vortex makes a vector. It is so efficient, so focused, I'm reminded of hunting spells. These poems are like conversations with spirits. They are summoning the ghosts of animals and perfect kills are being promised. Certainly, if I were an ibex, I would be doomed already by the force of their descriptions.

I am used to reading poetry which is more impressionist. The English lyric tradition is moist, as if secreted by the tear duct. Poems spoken in the first person tend to come up clouded, mooded, pensive, confiding. "Whoso list to hunt, I know where is an hind, but as for me, alas, I may no more . . ." I have trained myself on Wyatt's faltering voice. I was not prepared for the will-powered exactness of these poems.

From threnodies which include the deaths of animals, through various portraits of wild creatures in flight and humans in chase, to a prose account of a day's coursing in the mountains, this book traces the evolution of a genre: the *ṭardiyyah* or hunting poem. A genre, like a secondhand shoe, never completely fits the wearer. Nevertheless, by connecting one poetry to another, it allows us to salute something utterly new, utterly strange, while also finding it familiar. Isn't the *ṭardiyyah* a bit like the lament for Enkidu? Isn't it comparable to the Inuit songs collected by Rasmussen? Isn't it exactly what Hughes was describing in *Poetry in the Making*, when he spoke of "The special kind of excitement, the slightly mesmerized and quite involuntary concentration with which you make out the stirrings of a new poem in your mind, then the outline, the mass and colour and clean final form of it in the midst of the general lifelessness, all that is too familiar to mistake. This is hunting and the poem is a new species of creature, a new specimen of the life outside your own." (Hughes, 1967)

Hughes' hunting poems—schooled in the disciplines of fishing and shooting—have the same fierceness as many of the poems in this book. The hawk, sitting with eyes closed in the top of a wood in Lupercal is not so different from the goshawk sitting on the wrist of al-Shamardal:

"Just before sunrise,
 I cross the dark,
 hoping for a lucky day
 with a curve-beaked gos
 clad in chain mail, last
 fed yesterday, hungrily
 scanning the pool at Ṭams
 and beyond with an irate stare
 or the eyes of a man in fever's

grip. When cast, she spots
twenty dusty houbaras,
waddling like women, backs
bent with bundles of firewood,
or like Christians in dark robes . . ."

But what does it mean to compare an eighth-century Arabic poem with a twentieth-century English one? Poets of the *ṭardiyyāt* were building a poetics by responding to each other's work and for that reason, even in a selection which spans two centuries, there is a kinship between their poems. As far as I know, Ted Hughes was not familiar with al-Shamardal's poetry. If a hawk marks the place where his gaze crosses al-Sharmadal's, then the similarities are worth noticing. But I am more interested in their differences!

Hughes pursues animals in order to catch Poetry itself and Poetry for Hughes is a goddess, who "cannot come all the way....she comes as far as water, no further . . .

She comes dumb she cannot manage words
She brings petals in their nectar fruits in their plush
She brings a cloak of feathers an animal rainbow
She brings her favorite furs and these are her speeches . . ."

Throughout his work, Hughes is hunting this impossible female, whose presence, just beyond his poems, gives them a slight theatricality. Hughes' creatures seem to yearn beyond themselves. Like a set of characters in a mystery play, they emerge in dialogue and they have a certain charisma and courtliness, even in their violence. What surprises me about the *ṭardiyyāt,* at least in this translation, is the way the poems lead you to a giddying emptiness. Beyond the ibex, beyond the ostrich and the houbaras, even beyond the humans and the gods, the poems are facing something purely impersonal—which is Fate.

The word is *al-Dahr*. According to the translator, a more precise definition of *al-Dahr* is Time. Fate is a character, who might be appeased by humans, but Time is nothing. It is simply the law by which we move through moments, one of which will be our last. Between the present moment and the first moment after death, there is a blind spot—as inaccessible to thought as a blink is invisible to an eye. The blindspot cannot be known but it can be mimicked—and that is what these poems seem to me to achieve: they capture Time by means of mimicry. . . .

> "Death has laid Abū 'Amr on the highlands beneath a heap of
> stones . . .
> Why weep? Fate hunts the full-grown ibex in his glade
> under wisps of clouds unwound like turbans. . . .
> . . .
> Fate hunts the majestic
> supple-winged eagle who rests her two fledglings on a bed
> of hare flesh, the hearts of birds stored inside her nest like date
> pits discarded by a reveler . . ."

Like a film of last moments, the poem moves closer and closer to its subject without quite touching what it seeks: from a man to an ibex to the flesh of a hare to the small hearts of birds to scattered date-pits—each death creates its own scale, magnifies its moment, and delivers a shot of pain, as if the aim was not to soften us with comforts, but to harden us with glances. Hughes has a hard glance, but he fires it at characters not nothingness.

In their original language, the *ṭardiyyāt* are highly wrought, each line a syntactical unit sealed by a mono-rhyme and perhaps these patterns mollify their message. According to his introduction, James Montgomery experimented with equivalent forms in English but he decided that the results were too rigid. In particular, he felt that the "hegemony of the line" made his versions "inert and onerous." Montgomery has written elsewhere about translation being successful insofar as it doesn't try to keep everything. He calls it an act of "trauma" in which "loss" is fundamental to the process and this is a useful image for thinking about the genre itself—which, in its mixture of scrutiny and compassion, is really a free translation from animal language into human. Two species exchange selves by means of mimicry. The death of a human matches the death of an ibex, the death of an oryx, the death of an onager. The pace of an ostrich feels like a bucket slipping from the water carrier's grasp when a rope snaps. Twenty dusty houbaras waddle like women "backs bent with bundles of firewood." The simile stands between them like a simultaneous interpreter and the pain of the poem is generated by this very close but always imperfect likeness between species. I might even say (without knowing any Arabic) that the insights which connect predator and prey are continued and intensified by the insights which connect a good translation to its text. Which is another way of saying that a good translator (and Montgomery is a very good translator) has to intuit the animal's thoughts as well as the original poet's.

I think that's why, over and over again, I found myself thinking of Homer, who meets the trauma of the *Iliad* through the pain of not quite matching similes, many of which dramatize the tension between predator and prey:

> "Like an eagle, peering this way and that,
> they call it the sharpest-sighted
> of all upward things under the sky,
> whose highest eye, the quick-footed hare
> in a leafy thicket can't hide from
> when it suddenly plummets to the kill . . ."

Death in the *Iliad* speaks a trans-language between human, animal, arboreal, mineral, and meteorological. A man dies and the darkness clouds his eyes and he falls like a tower, he falls like a diver, he falls like a shock of corn . . . blood spreads like dye on the cheek guard of a horse and one man murders another like a lion leaping on the neck of an ox, or he falls on the enemy like wind battering the waves, or like a hawk cutting through starlings, or like dogs harrying a deer...and a head sinks over like a poppy under a rain shower, and a man falls like a black poplar growing in the marshes, with just a few branches at the top when someone cuts it down to make a chariot wheel . . .

When you read a simile in the *Iliad*, you are already pre-programmed by the similarity which shapes the whole poem: in Book 24, Priam and Achilles are on opposite sides but they discover something in common. The *Iliad* redresses difference. If one man kills another like a lion leaping on the neck of an ox, then something is given back when Achilles grieves for Patroclus, like a lion whose cubs have been stolen . . .

No doubt there are comparable qualities in the *ṭardiyyāt*, but they are not what makes this book essential reading for anyone who loves poetry. I want to praise it for a flavor which I can't quite define, because I have not really encountered it before, but its trace is definitely here in this rained-on house in Bristol, long after I put the book down and I think it is to do with unredressed difference. When (Poem 22) an ostrich lifts its neck like a banner on a bargeman's pole and shakes its tent-like wings clenched together as tightly as a miser's fist and runs as fast as a well bucket slipping from the water carrier's grasp, when it shakes like a halfwit and sleeps like a tent tied to its pegs and swallows food like a snake digesting a lump and moves like a shock of white hair on a dark collar or a star fired at a rebellious devil tumbling from the sky and finally crashes to the ground like a pack camel laden with gear. . . . then identity is secondary to movement and the self itself is called into question. These similes will not resolve their differences. Like a series of blinks, they cannot be known, only mimicked and that's why I will have to conclude this introduction not with a conclusion but with a simile.

I remember once I walked the streets of Paris, looking for a particular flavor. I was with a poet from Syria, who claimed that the scent of the Kurdish mountains could be tasted in a certain drink called arak. It is made of fermented grapes and aniseed, but in his description, I detected other flavors: myrtle and boxwood, broom, tamarisk, lemon and panic grass, black boulders and ibex and mirage. Arak is distilled in copper vessels, then left to age in clay jars and the part which evaporates is called "the angel's share," implying that in summer a thin layer of arak ascends in the heat haze and angels float about with bottles collecting it. We never found that drink. But not long after my return to England, a parcel arrived containing six volumes of Arabic poetry, including these pre-Islamic hunting poems. It is not that I want to compare the poems to arak, but perhaps the sense I have that a poetics beyond my knowledge has passed through me and has something in common with the evaporation of a drink I've never tasted, which can only be collected elsewhere by the angels or the jinn or the ghosts of hunted animals.

Alice Oswald
Bristol, England

Introduction

The poets of pre-Islamic Arabia (ca. AD 500–622), or the Jahiliya, lived in a world in which they were hunted by Fate. Fate, and its avatar Death, stalked them remorselessly: ready, like a hunter, to spring an ambush or, like a predator, to launch an attack. The hunt emerges in the poetry of the period as a central conceptual matrix within which the worth of men and the value of their deeds are assessed and turned into song. A successful kill represented a temporal climax in which the hunter, through the skilled management of the hunting team (huntsmen, falconers, raptors, salukis, even cheetahs), mimicked and appropriated the workings of Fate—a fleeting instant in which the hunter was master of his identity.

With the advent of Islam, this matrix was eventually fine-tuned, but it persisted without much alteration—it was now God who set man's destiny. The hunt continued to fulfill its functions as a means of subsistence, as an important regal and ritual ceremony (the ruler as feeder of his people), and as a way of interpreting existence. A genre of poetry emerged in which this hunting complex was explored and celebrated, known in Arabic as the *ṭardiyyah* (pl. *ṭardiyyāt*), literally the poem of the chase or hunt.[1]

The Hunting Complex

The easiest way to appreciate the role the hunting complex plays in the earliest Arabic poetry is to consider the *marthiyah*, the threnody or funeral song. We find a fine example in what is probably one of the oldest Arabic poems extant, by al-Muraqqish al-Akbar, Poem 4 in this volume.

ʿAmr ibn Mālik al-Muraqqish belonged to a clan of the powerful Bakr ibn Wāʾil super-tribe. Al-Muraqqish's family were renowned for their poets: his father was a famous poet, three of his nephews were prominent poets, and he was great-uncle to the composer of one of the *Muʿallaqāt* ("Suspended Odes") and cousin to the composer of another. This poem connects him with the power struggle in the first half of the sixth century between the Kindite kings of Ḥajr (modern-day Riyadh) and the Lakhmid rulers of Ḥīrah. Al-Muraqqish died ca. AD 550.

The poem is addressed to a powerful overlord, and presents a case in defense of the poet's tribe, which was apparently accused of involvement in a raid. It includes a lament for the poet's kinsman, whose corpse lies unburied on the field of battle, presumably a casualty in the raid described in the second half of the poem. The lament features a sequence in which an ibex, one of the qasida's iconic nonhumans, dies.

If anything could escape Fate, the bearded,
white-striped ibex on ʿAmāyah ridge
or on Mount Khiyam could. He almost touches the sky,
higher than an aerie, on the slopes of a mighty
broad-backed peak where he ranges at will.
Had Death overlooked him, he'd have grown old—
but Fate struck and he slipped and fell to his death.

The notion of the inexorability of Fate is taken up by two poets from the tribe of Hudhayl, part of the southern Arabian (Ḥijāzī) rather than the northern Arabian (Najdī) poetic tradition. Here is the ibex scene from a funeral song by Ṣakhr al-Ghayy, Poem 6 in this volume.

One day, after many years of life, Fate confronts it
with the youngest son of a shaykh bent with age and starving,

who shelters his father in winter and zealously forages fruit
for him in summer, like a man pleading his case before a judge.
He spots the ibex and exclaims, "By God! Who's seen a white-
leg as big as this in our day? It'll keep our father
alive until the stars bring the rains." He stalks him
and at close range fires a hard arrow with a cleft head,
true to its aim. Shouting to his brother, he closes in with a knife
and briskly butchers the ibex.

Fate also destroys the "supple-winged eagle" in this threnody, the concluding verses of which are:

Such are the workings of Fate—
master of both hunter and fleet-footed prey.

Several decades later, in a *marthiyah* for his sons who had died of the plague in Egypt while participating in the Islamic conquests, Abū Dhu'ayb describes three victims of Fate in his poem (Poem 9 in this volume): the onager jack with his harem, the solitary oryx buck, and two iconic warriors:

both lie dead
from wounds like rips in cloth beyond repair.
They lived for glory and fame—but why?

The cosmos of the pre-Islamic qasida poets is stark. Everything is governed by Fate (or Time, *al-Dahr*) and Death. Fate is the supreme hunter, and all that exists, human and nonhuman, is its quarry. At the heart of the cosmos stands man, either alone, or with his family or his kin group, or both. The cosmos was unpredictable: A man knew that it could and would inevitably infect him, his honor, and his society with a most terrifying disease: disunity and disintegration. What he did not know was when this would happen. The inevitability of Fate rendered this unpredictability and the human responses to it all the more urgent. The events of this cosmos play out in the desert, the landscape where a man on camelback pits himself against Time and risks his all in a series of actions whose outcomes are determined solely by chance.[2]

The hunting complex is an obvious intonation of this stark cosmos. The human hunters it describes enjoy success and suffer failure. The nonhumans they hunt may escape or be killed. For the human hunters, success is an opportunity for a temporary and vicarious emulation of Fate, but the hunt is unpredictable and short-lived—its victory is both a respite from and a reminder of the hunter's vulnerability and mortality.

Central to the poetics of what I am referring to as "the hunting complex" is the crystalline clarity of the poet's eye—whereby the nonhumans really come to life. The way in which the poems dissect reality on a micro scale makes us witness to a process that magnifies subtler and subtler distinctions within the real (to evoke Roland Barthes's appreciation of the haiku).[3] In the meticulous attention paid by the poets to the stages of the hunt, the chase, and the kill, these poems blur distinctions between the perceptions of the poet as hunter and the perceptions of the nonhumans. The poems thus offer us both a micro-scale conceptualization of relationality and a blurring, at the phenomenological level, of the human and nonhuman, mediated by the poet, who is simultaneously participant, observer, and creator.

In this way, many of our poems blur the distinctions between human and nonhuman. I consider this blurred perspective to be as indicative of the Arabic poetic aesthetic as the micro-scale conceptualization of relationality. This phenomenological blurring was a special feature of the classical poetic tradition, similar to the representational strategies encountered in other Arabic poetic genres.

In his article "Medieval Blood Sport," William Marvin discusses with great insight the "depths of experience with animal consciousness among medieval hunters," noting the delicate balance that is required for a successful hunt in which "the ferocity of the hunting instinct" must be spurred in "the animal team" until it reaches a critical point and results in a kill, at which point the discipline of training is required in order "to halt . . . (the) destruction of the prey."[4] In order to achieve and maintain this balance, in order to catch the quarry, the hunter must enter into a deep and "instinctual . . . familiarity" with the prey as well as with the hunting team. All three—human hunter, nonhuman hunter, and nonhuman prey—enter, in Marvin's words,

> the same phenomenology by having to (a) register sudden stimuli, (b) assess the level of threat, (c) process the immediate time-distance-ground problems, and (d) execute the run with maximum potential for speed and stratagem.[5]

He refers to the attendant "powers of hyper-focus" and notes that the hunt endows "lesser-seeming creatures" with "superpowers."[6] Therefore, a phenomenon that might have seemed particular to the Arabic poetic aesthetic turns out, in essence, to belong to a widespread phenomenology of the hunt. And the micro-scale conceptualization of relationality that is often considered typical of the classical Arabic poetic tradition becomes, in the context of the *ṭardiyyah*, an index of Marvin's "hyper-focus."

I consider the process of converting into verbal and poetic form the experience of this phenomenology and relationality to be an act of translation, in the sense that, for example, we could argue that language is an act of translation. These poems, therefore, offer us an insight into how the phenomenology of the hunting complex is communicated and shared by being translated into verse.

Nonhuman Hunters

Our poets rarely name the nonhuman hunters. Rather than saying, for example, "I went on an expedition with a saker," they prefer to say, "I went on an expedition with a trim, rufous (noun absent)." That is, they take it for granted that the audience knows exactly which type of nonhuman they intend. My suspicion is that they also expect their audience to know exactly which individual bird or dog they intend. I suspect further that the nonhuman was present to hear and perhaps somehow to understand the poem, though this is just a hunch.

This can pose some intractable problems for us today. It is perhaps a relief to see that the learned scholars of the past who knew so much about the poetry and who wrote comments on these poems also struggled sometimes to identify the nonhumans properly. In fact, I think on one or two occasions they may have gotten it wrong. Thus, while these poems were not intended by their creators to function as riddles, they have become riddles with the passage of the centuries.

The following twenty-six poems and one prose poem in the form of an epistle describe the following nonhuman raptors: *ṣaqr*: the saker falcon (*Falco cherrug*); *shāhīn*: the peregrine falcon (*Falco peregrinus*); *bāz*: the goshawk (*Accipiter gentilis*); and *laqwah*: Bonelli's eagle (*Aquila fasciata*).[7] Several four-legged hunters also feature in the chase: dogs, presumably the saluki; cheetahs (*Acinonyx jubatus*); and horses. A good number of our poems feature a solitary hunter armed with bow and arrow.

The poems from the earliest period contain no descriptions of falconry, the practice of hunting with trained raptors; the horse and the hound are the trained nonhuman hunters of pre-Islamic Arabia. The earliest poems in which hawking features date from the middle of the Umayyad period (ca. AD 700). The cheetah *ṭardiyyah* by Abū l-Najm is probably from the first quarter of the eighth century, and it is to ʿAbd al-Ḥamīd al-Kātib that we owe the earliest references to hunting with sakers and peregrines.

As a genre, the corpus of *ṭardiyyāt* contains more poems about hunting with saluki hounds than with any other creature, and more poems about hunting with the goshawk than with the falcon. The record is not reliable (we are, after all, dealing with the vagaries of chance survival), but I am tempted to suggest that it was harder to acquire falcons than hawks, and harder to acquire raptors than dogs.

The Hunted

Which nonhumans were hunted? The answer to this depends to an extent on the terrain on which the hunting expedition took place and the kind of nonhuman hunter that formed part of the hunting team. We encounter general mentions of desert plains, rivers, and water holes, including oases, woodlands, shrublands, mountain ravines, wadis, lakes, and ponds. It is also possible that the so-called paradise (*jannah*), the game reserve managed for hunting expeditions, was used.

I have counted around twenty different kinds of quarry in the *ṭardiyyāt* as a genre. But the quarry is not mentioned or described in every poem, so sometimes we don't know exactly what, for example, the goshawk hunted and caught. And there are additional challenges in identifying the quarry even when it is referred to in the corpus.

The first challenge—the riddle that besets our attempts to identify the nonhuman hunter—holds doubly true for the hunted nonhuman. In other words, the riddles are even more demanding and baffling when we seek to know exactly which hunted nonhumans are meant.

The second challenge is that these nonhumans are rarely the primary focus of the poet's attention. So even when the poet names, say, a gazelle or a *ẓaby*, we still do not know precisely which type of gazelle is meant. To confine my remarks only to the saker and the peregrine, we hear of the following prey: houbaras (*Chlamydotis macqueenii*), hares (*Lepus capensis*), and gazelles and *ẓaby*s. But do the poets mean the dorcas gazelle (*Gazella dorcas*); the Arabian mountain gazelle (*Gazella gazella cora*), sometimes referred to as the idmi gazelle; or the slender-horned gazelle (*Gazella arabica*), sometimes referred to as the rhim gazelle? I am afraid I don't know the answer. The poets also say that the saker and the peregrine hunt teal (*burkah*)—that is, the Eurasian teal (*Anas crecca*); waterfowl (*ṭayr al-māʾ*), presumably the mallard—that is, the wild duck (*Anas platyrhynchos*); the northern bald ibis (*Geronticus eremita*) (*bughth*); the partridge (*ḥajal* or *dayzaj*),[8] either the see-see partridge (*Ammoperdix griseogularis*) or the sand partridge (*Ammoperdix heyi*); and the chukar (*Alectoris chukar*), a favorite quarry of falcons.

The poets also tell us that the saker and peregrine catch geese. But does the word *iwazz* refer to the greater white-fronted goose (*Anser albifrons*), the lesser white-fronted goose (*Anser erythropus*), the greylag goose (*Anser anser*), or the red-breasted goose (*Branta ruficolis*)?

Human Hunters

Can we get any information from the poems about who carried out the hunting? We might naturally want to assume the poets were the hunters, but this is not always the case. Some poems describe the poet as conducting the hunt, while others describe a falconer or an austringer or a huntsman, say a master of hounds or a cheetah handler, who accompanies the expedition.

The answer is connected with which nonhuman hunters were used. In the case of the saluki sight hound, many poems in the *ṭardiyyah* genre concern fairly ordinary people who live off whatever their dogs can catch. But in this corpus we also meet, for example, a saluki owned by the caliph al-Amīn (r. 193–98/809–13). In the case of the cheetah, we must expect that only the elite could afford to hunt with such a creature.

Much of the language of the hunt and many of the adjectives used to convey falconry practices in particular reveal a Persian origin. I think it likely that many of the practices, techniques, and traditions of the hunt were inflections of what Thomas Allsen has identified as the royal Eurasian hunt.[9] But the hunting practices of the Arabian Peninsula, coursing onager and oryx with horse and saluki, and hunting with the bow and arrow, are also featured, especially in the early corpus.

The Royal Hunt and the Subsistence Hunt

The poems collected here showcase two types of hunt: Allsen's "royal hunt," and what we can refer to as the subsistence hunt—that is, hunting conducted with a view to securing the food needed for the survival of an individual or a group. As examples of subsistence hunting, we have the solitary, often destitute hunter, armed with his bow and arrows (whom we encounter, for example, in Poems 6, 8, and 10), and the hunter with his hounds (Poem 7). Examples of the royal hunt are furnished by Poems 1 and 6 and by the prose poem of ʿAbd al-Ḥamīd. Harder to categorize are the poems that represent the early stages of the *ṭardiyyah* as a genre: Poems 8–14 and 16. They feature the goshawk and so belong to what we might refer to as the Asiatic (as opposed to the Arabian) hunt. I am inclined to interpret these too as inflections of the royal hunt.[10]

The royal hunt was an elite enterprise, with symbolic, ceremonial, and political significance. It was frequently conducted on a lavish scale, and often in a paradise, a park constructed, managed, and cultivated for hunting. As Allsen notes, it portrayed the ability of a ruler to govern through the marshaling of "labor, military manpower, and individuals (both humans and animals) with very special skills." It was central to "interstate relations, military preparations, domestic administration, communications networks, and . . . the search for political legitimacy" and it required the "preservation of natural resources."[11]

In our corpus, we encounter two types of subsistence hunting: killing prey with bow and arrow, and chasing quarry with dogs. There is no mention in the texts from the pre-Islamic period of other types of subsistence hunting such as hawking or trapping birds with nets or snares. This is a reminder, if one was needed, that our poems are representations, rather than documentations, of events. The poems eloquently demonstrate that "fabulous beasts can only be slain by fabulous humans."[12]

These types of hunt are distinguished primarily in terms of scale, rather than in terms of goals—after all, a royal hunt would often culminate in a feast on the quarry secured in the progress of the hunt, and the subsistence hunt, as the destitute hunters of al-Muzarrid's and al-Ḥuṭay'ah's poems remind us (Poems 8 and 10, respectively), was also a matter of social status and position within the group. Presumably, both a subsistence hunt and a royal hunt would also have been an occasion for the pursuit of pleasure.

Fate the Hunter

Fate the Hunter is the first installment in a series of volumes I am editing and translating that feature the *ṭardiyyah* from its origins in the pre-Islamic period to the era of al-Mutanabbī (d. 354/965) and Abū Firās (d. 357/968). In order to keep the corpus focused, I have decided not to extend this to the development of the genre in the Mamluk era or the emergence in later centuries of the hunting epistle-cum-prose poem in *saj*ʿ (prose with rhyme and rhythm).[13] Future volumes will include the hunting poetry of Abū Nuwās (d. 199/813) and Ibn al-Muʿtazz (d. 296/908), and will conclude with a miscellany of hunting poems from the second/eighth to the fourth/tenth centuries. My aim is not to be exhaustive, but comprehensive and representative.

Fate the Hunter includes editions and translations of twenty-six poems that I have selected not with a view to providing an account of the origins and development of the *ṭardiyyah* as a genre, but rather to exploring some of the early semiotic and thematic contours of the hunting complex that later *ṭardiyyāt* looked to and drew from.[14] They include three poems that do not contain what we would classify strictly as hunting scenes when considered in terms of the genre. I chose these poems both for their descriptions of nonhumans and for how they are informed by and predicated upon the hunting complex. They also happen to be poems I am especially fond of.

Of these twenty-six poems, seven are from the Jahiliya; three are by *mukhaḍram* poets—that is, those who straddled the latter stages of the Jahiliya and the early Islamic era; and sixteen date to the second half of the Umayyad era. All in all, thirteen poets are represented. The selection concludes with a translation of the earliest extant prose epistle (*risālah*) on the hunt, by ʿAbd al-Ḥamīd al-Kātib (d. 135/750), addressed to a caliph, either Hishām ibn ʿAbd al-Malik (r. 105–25/724–43) or Marwān II (r. 127–33/744–50).

*

My first encounter with a *ṭardiyyah* occurred in 1987. I had been reading the poetry of Abū Firās al-Ḥamdānī, contemporary of al-Mutanabbī and composer of the *Rūmiyyāt*, the series of poems he wrote from his captivity in Byzantium while he waited for his cousin Sayf al-Dawlah to pay his ransom. Abū Firās has one long poem composed in *rajaz* meter that describes a hunting expedition. I vividly remember my bewilderment at its lexicon. When I could locate a lexical item in dictionaries and lexica, I was confronted with a further problem—my complete ignorance of the nonhuman that the word signified. I had no clue about the difference between a hawk and a falcon, let alone the difference between a goshawk and a sparrow hawk, or a saker and a peregrine falcon. And because I knew nothing about these raptors or about how they hunted, to say nothing of what animals they were trained to hunt, I could make neither head nor tail of the events of the poem. The situation improved greatly with the publication in 1990 of Rex Smith's brilliant survey "Hunting Poetry (*Ṭardiyyāt*)" in the second volume of *The Cambridge History of Arabic Literature, ʿAbbāsid Belles-Lettres*.

Armed with Smith's insights, I felt emboldened to write an article on Abū Firās's poem, published in 1999 as "Abū Firās's Veneric *Urjūzah Muzdawijah*." The research I carried out for that article included reading the *ṭardiyyāt* of Abū Nuwās and Ibn al-Muʿtazz, and this sowed the germ of an ambition to work more closely on them. These plans were frustrated, however. In the dark days before the internet, it was impossible to acquire detailed information about the habits of raptors, for example, or the techniques of falconry—short of taking up the sport myself, of course, or seeking to befriend an expert. But anyway, by this stage al-Jāḥiẓ had started to colonize my mind and I forgot all about the *ṭardiyyāt*.

And so things continued, until December 2012, when, on a visit to the Abu Dhabi Falcon Hospital, I came across the following poem by Shaykh Zayed bin Sultan Al Nahyan (d. 2004):

My bird, I've trained
    and tested you. Now
I challenge you—stoop
    to the kill, bind to
in the air when the dusty
    houbaras, big
as ostriches, fly
    from the branches in fear.
Please do not fail.
    Chase the leader,
attack the head,
    ruthless like the wolf—
you won't be bested.
    Let the winds bring
the scattered feathers
    from the kill! Care
for your bird or you'll regret
    flying her—you'll call
and shout in vain.
    Brothers and friends,
watch and judge
    how she performs.
Send the jeep
    if she's not back by night.
Prepare provisions.

Note the drama of this poem. Shaykh Zayed describes that most tense of moments: the first flight of a newly trained falcon. Will the bird perform well? Will she prove to be a skilled hunter? Will she make a kill? Will she survive the first hunt uninjured? Will she take to the wing and not return?[15] Crucially, will the falcon's performance redound to the credit of her trainer and hunter? The shaykh's hunting party and companions are on hand, watching, ready to assess not only how well the bird flies but how well she has been trained.

The dramatic success of the poem lies in the fact that we are not told the outcome. We hope the hunt is successful, but the poet does not tell us the result of this maiden flight. Clive Holes, whom I consulted in order to understand the poem, suggested that it may also address other concerns. He proposed that it is possibly a meditation on leadership and maybe even nationhood, with the close relationship between poet-hunter and falcon a symbol for the care and attention with which the Father of the Nation leads his people.

The poem is cleverly constructed. The hunt and kill are described in the form of a wish, as an instruction to the novice bird; then the aftermath of the kill is imagined. Reflections on success and failure lead to the expectation of the traditional feast at the end of the hunt, though in this poem the feast may be postponed while the hunting expedition searches for the falcon. This structure is basically a modification of one of the patterns we encounter in the hunting poems from the classical tradition.

And so a chance encounter with a poem a decade ago led me to revisit an earlier project, the first fruits of which are contained in this book.

*

In her Preface to T. H. White's *The Goshawk*, a tale about White's "exercise of power" while attempting to train a hawk, with disastrous effects, Helen Macdonald, author of the celebrated *H Is for Hawk*, laments "humanity's . . . inability to see nature as anything other than a mirror of ourselves."[16] The nonhumans we encounter in the *ṭardiyyāt* are ultimately no exception to this. But at the same time, they afford us a glimpse into how, in the hunting complex, the distinction between human and nonhuman becomes blurred: the human, in order to achieve his goal, is forced to enter the consciousness of the nonhuman.

This is akin to what some critics consider to be profoundly modern in recent poetry concerning the human-nonhuman encounter. The poet and critic John Hollander notes how, in their poems about nonhumans, modern poets tend to focus on a "particular encounter between a human person and an animal presence, generating fables of a more complex sort than mere emblems."[17] It is the ambiguity, and even the alterity, of the encounter with nonhumans as described in these poems that keep drawing me back. I hope this volume will encourage readers to open themselves up to the *ṭardiyyah*'s magnificent visions of the nonhuman.

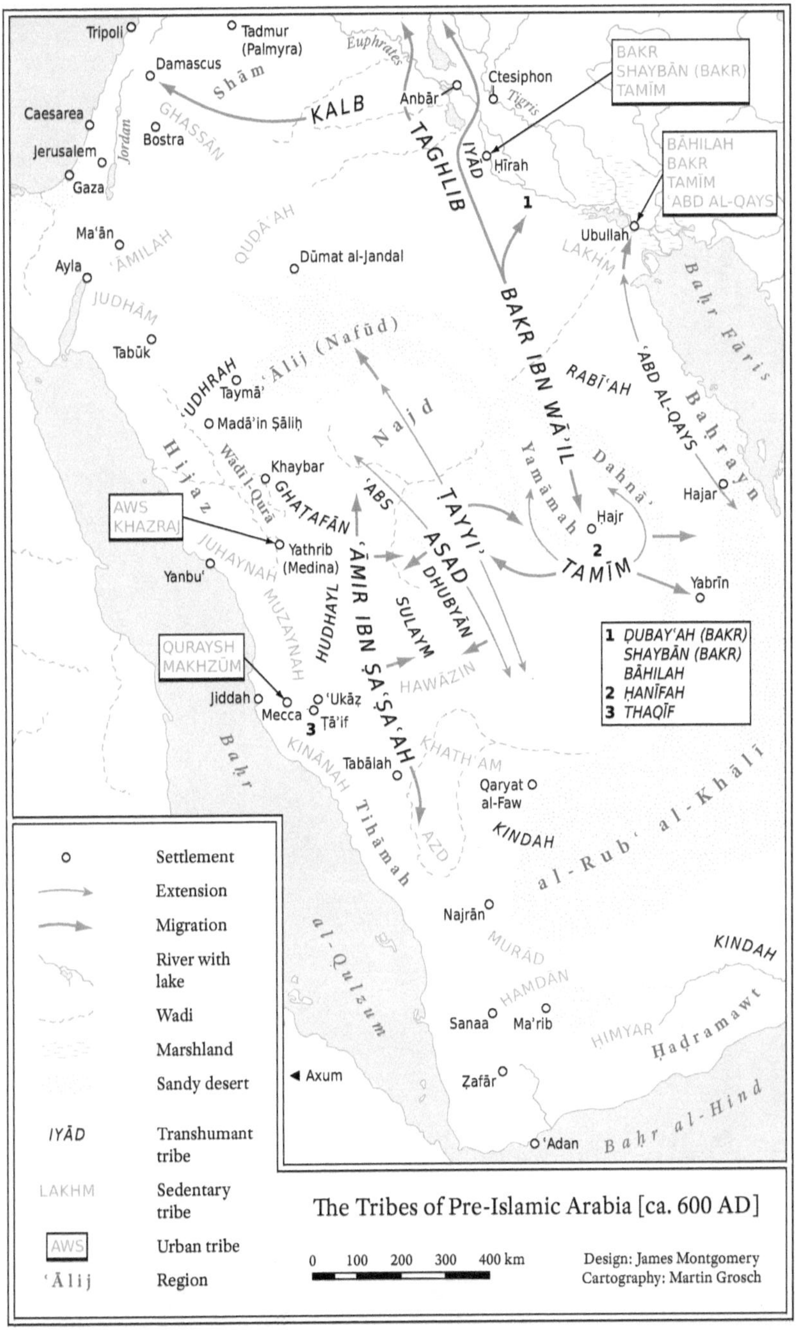

The Tribes of Pre-Islamic Arabia [ca. 600 AD]

Note on the Text

One of the central tenets of the Library of Arabic Literature is to publish *textes intégrales*—that is, books (or chapters in books) that existed as identifiable, contained formats in the premodern tradition, rather than publishing excerpts or selections from a text. Therefore, this book is unusual for an LAL volume in that it is a selection of texts that does not already exist as an anthology in the premodern tradition. I am grateful to the editors for acceding to my arguments and allowing me to create the book. It is intended to set the stage for the subsequent volumes of *tardiyyāt* currently in preparation. So I based my principle of selection on two objectives: to outline the contours of the pre-Islamic and Umayyad poetic traditions from which later poets might have drawn, and to suggest the centrality of what I have termed the hunting complex, not only to the *ṭardiyyah*, but to the classical Arabic poetic imaginary.

I have not tried to make my selection exhaustive, but rather comprehensive and representative. There are many more hunting scenes in pre-Islamic qasidas than the smattering I present here, and I have omitted the Umayyad *qaṣīd* tradition almost entirely (with the exception of Poem 23), concentrating instead on the exiguous remains of Umayyad *ṭardiyyāt* composed in *mashṭūr al-rajaz*, almost the most constant feature of the genre in its developed Abbasid form. This is why the book contains no qasidas by poets such as al-Akhṭal and Dhū l-Rummah. I have also omitted, from the project as a whole, the rich tradition of Mamluk hunting poetry and epistolography (on which, see Thomas Bauer, "The

Dawādār's Hunting Party: A Mamluk *Muzdawija Ṭardiyya*, probably by Shihāb al-Dīn Ibn Faḍl Allāh"). It should also be noted that many of the poems I have selected include scenes that were not taken up in the developed genre, such as those in which an indigent hunter, concealed in a hide, ambushes a herd of onagers as they arrive at a water hole. In many of these vignettes, however, descriptions of the bow and arrows used by the hunter play a significant role and as such are intimations of later hunting poems that depict the use of the pellet bow.

My selection is also idiosyncratic and impressionistic. I have chosen poems that I like, and several (Poems 2, 3, and 5) do not contain hunting scenes in any proper sense. One of the reasons I decided to include them was the poeticality and power of their description of nonhumans. They are, moreover, insightful and instructive inflections of the hunting complex, especially in the case of Poem 5, in which the poet al-Shanfarā becomes the quarry hunted by his crimes, which are personified and portrayed in a manner not dissimilar to the ancient Greek goddesses of vengeance, the Erinyes (the Furies).

One feature of the book should be noted. Short biographies of each poet and appreciations of each piece are to be found in the section "Note on the Poems." In order to keep the translation as uncluttered as possible, I have avoided annotation and have provided as an addendum to my discussion of each poem such notes and remarks as were absolutely necessary. I have also used this opportunity to refer the reader to pertinent studies of the poems, when available, and to a handful of poems, predominantly in English, that can be read (with enjoyment, I hope) alongside my versions.

The Translation

A constant challenge in trying to translate a poem is the presence of formal features in the source language that are absent in the target language. In the case of Classical Arabic poetry, there are two principal formal features: terminal monorhyme, whereby each line of a poem concludes with the same consonant and its attendant vowel, and meter, whereby each line of a poem is composed in the same meter throughout. Less immediately prominent, but no less important, are rhetorical features, such as wordplay, antithesis, and paronomasia, to name just three. There is a third principal formal feature that often goes unremarked. Classical Arabic poems are made up of lines that are almost always syntactically and semantically self-contained, and therefore apparently autonomous of the other lines in the poem.[18] Poetic meaning is thus generated through parataxis, rather than through enjambment and hypotaxis (whence the notion of "orient pearls at random strung," as Sir William Jones (d. 1794) rendered a line by Hafez (d. 792/1390)).[19]

Most translations of Arabic poetry (whatever their ambition, scholarly or literary) will dispense with terminal monorhyme and meter, but few disregard the hegemony of the line. And many readers of English translations of this poetry who are familiar with the Arabic of the source texts will object vociferously to any attempts to disregard this hegemony.

In my work as a translator of Classical Arabic poems, I have found, however, that it is the hegemonic line that has presented the sternest challenge. This held true in the early stages of this book: my first drafts of Poems 1 to 9 were attempts to develop in English a single line, of varying stress, that might accommodate the source texts, but without resorting to the two-step line, in which the hemistichs of the source texts are by and large preserved. The experiment proved unsatisfactory to both my ear and my eye: the poems looked as if they were hewn from granite and sounded just as heavy. This is not how I hear these Arabic poems. To be sure, they have an impressive monumentality and an imposing sonority, but they are definitely not inert or onerous. They pulse with energy and luxuriate in their distinctive sound patterns. My adherence to the formal feature of the autonomous line had succeeded merely in distorting the vitality of that feature.

When I reread Tennyson's "Locksley Hall" (1842), inspired by his reading of the *Muʿallaqah* of Imruʾ al-Qays (Poem 1), I became intrigued by Tennyson's trochaic doublets of four feet per hemistich. Driven by the desire to capture the energy of the Arabic poems, I decided to impose a constraint upon my translations: the preservation of a loosely articulated but constant stress pattern throughout the whole translation. Poem 6 thus has a six-stress pattern and Poem 1 a five-stress pattern, while the versions translated from *rajaz* poems (Poems 11–26) alternate between three and four stresses per line. Interestingly, in *mashṭūr al-rajaz*, the version of the meter used by the poets, in which each "hemistich" forms an independent verse that rhymes with the preceding verses, the paratactical autonomy of the poems so prevalent in more formal meters is less pronounced. This I think is a result of the brevity of their "hemistichs."

By imposing this simple constraint, I was forced to embrace enjambment and endeavor to exploit its semantic possibilities. I discovered that I could try to listen for the poem, to create spaces for the energy of the source poems to burst through, for the concrete imagery to cascade before the mind's eye, thus acquiring potency through accumulation.

Notes to the Introduction

1 I am not a falconer or huntsman, or an expert in zoology. I am primarily interested in the poetics of this corpus, not in whether what the poets describe is consistent with animal behavior or ethology. I am only too aware that in my ignorance of and inexperience with the cynegetic art, I will have committed many an error, for which I apologize.

2 See further Montgomery, introduction to ʿAntarah ibn Shaddād, *War Songs*, xxix–xxxi.

3 See Briggs, *This Little Art*, 188.

4 Marvin, "Medieval Blood Sport," 57.

5 Marvin, "Medieval Blood Sport," 66.

6 Marvin, "Medieval Blood Sport," 68, 69.

7 In the current selection of poems, the eagle features as an independent predator, not as a trained hunter directed by a human, though it does appear in this latter capacity in a few later *ṭardiyyāt*.

8 The term *dayzaj* may also designate the cream-colored courser (*Cursorius cursor*).

9 Allsen, *The Royal Hunt in Eurasian History*.

10 Allen, *Falconry in Arabia*, 129. On the Umayyad hunt, see Brey, "The Caliph's Prey: Hunting in the Visual Cultures of the Umayyad Empire."

11 Allsen, *The Royal Hunt*, 8, 12.

12 Allsen, *The Royal Hunt*, 12.

13 On the Mamluk hunting poem, see Bauer, "The Dawādār's Hunting Party"; on the hunting *risālah*, see Hämeen-Anttila, *Maqama: A History of a Genre*, 213–15.

14 For overviews and literary histories of the genre, see al-Bāshā, *Shiʿr al-ṭarad ilā nihāyat al-qarn al-thālith al-hijrī*; al-Ṣāliḥi, *Al-Ṣayd wa-l-ṭarad fī al-shiʿr al-ʿarabī ḥattā nihāyat al-qarn al-thānī l-hijrī*; Wagner, *Grundzüge der klassischen arabischen Dichtung*, 2:46–58; Smith, "Hunting Poetry"; and Seidensticker, "Ṭardiyya."

15 See the two poems on the loss of a bird quoted and translated by Allen and Smith, "Some Notes on Hunting Techniques and Practices in the Arabian Peninsula," 145–46. The second of the three poems, from Najd, laments the loss of a bird not fully trained, in a manner similar to Shaykh Zayed's poem.

16 Macdonald, preface to White, *The Goshawk*, vi.

17 Hollander, "Animal Poems," 14.

18 See van Gelder, *Beyond the Line: Classical Arabic Literary Critics on the Coherence and Unity of the Poem.*

19 See van Ruymbeke, "Sir William Jones and the Anvar-e Sohayli."

Fate the Hunter

1

Imru' al-Qays: Echoes of Love Lost

Echoes of love lost where the dune dips 1.1
between Dakhūl and Ḥawmal, Tūḍiḥ and Miqrāt.
My tears brought the troop to a halt at the ruins,
faint, woven in patterns by the north and south
winds, grounds and pools spattered with rhim-
dung peppercorns. The day the tribe left,
I wept by the acacias, as if I'd crushed a wild gourd.
My comrades' camels towered over me: "Don't die of grief;
put on a brave face." "Can we trust ancient
ruins? Tears are my cure. They helped me recover
after Umm Ḥuwayrith and Umm Rabāb in Ma'sal,
a scent of musk like an aroma of cloves wafting
on an eastern breeze." So keen was my love, my eyes
wept hard and soaked the sword belt on my chest.

I've enjoyed many a precious day with women— 1.10
that day at Dārat Juljul, the day I slaughtered my camel
for the maidens who tossed about its meat and lumps
of fat like the fringes of a white silk cloth—
wondrous, to see my saddle carried away!
And the day I entered 'Unayzah's howdah.
Her camel lurched and threw us to one side. "Be careful!
You'll hock my beast and I'll have to walk. Get out,

Imru' al-Qays!" "Loosen the reins, let it walk on.
Don't deny me your delicious fruit. I've had women
like you, a pregnant mother with a child at her breast—
I brought her joy, made her forget her son
clad in his amulets; when he cried, she turned
toward him but kept her body pinned beneath me."

1.18 One day on the dune ridge, Fāṭimah resisted
and solemnly swore we were finished. "Slow down,
less flirtation," I urged. "If you've decided to break up,
please, be kind. But if it's something I've said
or done, untangle our clothes and we'll part ways.
Are you bold because your love destroys me and my heart
heeds your every command? These tears are meant
to cut me to the quick, a brave gamble to win
my murdered heart. I've had a woman, round, smooth
as an egg, hidden in a guarded tent—I took
my time; I enjoyed her to the full. To reach
her, I crept past sentries and kinsmen eager to boast
they'd killed me. The Pleiades in the night sky had moved
to the side, like the links of a body chain inlaid with gems
of alternating colors. She lay beside the screen, ready
for sleep, naked but for her shift. 'My God!' she cried.
'You can't succeed. I don't think you'll ever see
the error of your ways.' I took her from the tent, she covered
our tracks with the hem of a cloak decorated with saddle
designs. We crossed the court and reached the dip
of a wide, ridged valley. I cradled her head
and she yielded, her torso lean, slender, white,
her ankles plump, her chest burnished like a looking
glass. As she turned away she showed her cheek,
tender and smooth, her eyes wary like a Wajrah
doe tending to her fawn, her delicate throat,
clasped in a necklace, as graceful as a rhim's, her coal-

black hair, luxuriant, adorning her back
like date clusters tightly bunched on a palm,
her curls twisting upward, the plaits lost
in strands doubled and set loose, her lissome waist
thin as a leather strap, her legs like tall
well-watered date trees, racemes heavy with fruit.
She sleeps late, wearing only her shift, her bed
strewn with bruised musk grains, her fingers
soft and thin like the sandworms of Ẓaby
or *isḥil* tooth sticks. She brightens the dark
night like a monk's solitary lamp, too young
to dress in a gown, too old to wear a child's
frock—she makes grown men stare
with reckless desire. She's like an ostrich egg, white
with yellow dapplings, nourished by an unsullied stream.
Other lovers may find solace for their blind follies,
but my heart will never forget its passion!
Fāṭimah, for you I've faced so many rebukes
from mulish foes eager that I mend my ways."

A night swelling like the ocean waves put me 1.44
to the test with a myriad of cares. I watched it pass
like a camel stretching its spine, then its rump, then
heaving its chest from the ground. I said, "Begone,
never-ending night! Let day blaze forth, though dawn
won't find me free of your curse." The night was limitless,
the stars tied to Yadhbul by tightly twisted
ropes and the Seven Sisters fixed in their station,
fastened by flaxen cables to unyielding rock.

I've humbly carried the waterskins of many armies 1.49
slung on my shoulder. I've crossed wadis, flat
and empty like an onager's belly, where the wolf howls
like a gambler with a family to feed who's staked and lost
it all. "We're two of a pair," I answered his howl.

"We own little and we'll never get rich
by our gains. We lose every victory we win—
hunger awaits all who follow in our steps."

1.53 I cross the dark to hunt, the birds still asleep
in their nests, on a short-haired steed that catches the quarry
as it flees, as imposing as a temple, a whirl of motion,
onward, backward, wheeling, bolting, all
at once, swift as a huge boulder hurtled
from a height by a raging torrent. A bay, the numnah
sliding from his back like screes in a landslide. Battle-
hardened and spry—when fired up, his hooves pound
the ground, thrumming like a swiftly boiling cauldron.
When other racehorses kick up the sand and tire
in the arena, when flyweight jockeys are easily unseated
and the robes of the heavy rider flap and furl
behind him, my steed's pace is like a heavy downpour.
This horse is fleet and compact, like a boy's trompo
wound tight by twisting its string. His flanks
are like a *ẓaby*'s, like an ostrich his legs, like a wolf his lope,
like a fox cub his sprint, and his tail is long
and full, falling almost perfectly straight to the ground.
As he stands by my tent, his back is like a perfumer's mortar
or a stone for splitting gourds. Spattered across his neck,
the blood of the lead quarry is like henna juice
combed into white hair.

1.64 A herd of oryx now appeared,
the does like virgins at Dawār's shrine dressed
in bright gowns with black borders. The oryx
bolted, like a string of striated onyx on the neck
of a highborn child. The horse overtook the bull
at the head of the herd, before the rest had time to scatter,
and chased down, one by one, the bucks and does
without a drop of sweat lathering his hide.

Day-long, the cooks sizzled slabs of meat
on heated rocks or threw them into pots that boiled
fiercely. On the trip home, my eyes failed
to take in his size and grandeur. That night, saddled
up and bridled, he stood under my watchful gaze—
I refused to set him free to roam and graze.

Comrade, look! Can you see the lightning flash 1.71
from a cloud bank's huge crown, its brilliant
blast like two bright hands or a monk's lamps,
their twisted wicks drenched in oil? The troop
sat down to watch it, far away between Ḍārij and ʻUdhayb.
We saw the clouds release their flood above Qaṭan
to the right, while to the left the storm broke over Sitār
and Yadhbul. The next morning, the waters surged around Kutayfah,
forcing mighty *kanahbul* trees to the ground.
The debris swept over Qanān and drove the white-
leg ibex from their rocky homes, then moved
on to Taymā', toppling houses and palms—only towers
built of boulders remained. In the storm's early
bursts, Thabīr looked like an old man wrapped
in a striped blanket. Amid the flood and waste,
Mujaymir's crests were like the whorl of a weaver's spindle.
The tempest unleashed its load in the flat lands
like a Yemeni camel kneeling down, laden with heavy
baskets. At dawn the larks in the valleys sang
as if raucously drunk on vintage wine spiced
with peppercorns. At night, in the far reaches of the land,
drowned predators—wolves, lions, and hyenas—
floated, like uprooted sea onion bulbs.

2

ʿAbīd ibn al-Abraṣ: That Mighty Hunter the Eagle

2.1 Malḥūb, Quṭabiyyāt, Dhanūb,
Rākis, Thuʿālibāt, Dhāt Firqayn,
Qalīb, ʿArdah, Qafā Ḥibirr—now
deserted wastelands, the souls
who lived there gone, replaced
by wild beasts, lands destroyed
by Fate. Death who divides us
is heir to these domains
whose denizens died—or were slain.
Gray hair is a disgrace to age.
Tears stream from your eyes
like water gushing from a tattered
skin frayed at the seams
or a river rushing through steep
gullies or a spring gurgling
in a wadi or a stream shaded
by palms. You're a flood of emotion.
Why these feelings, frightened
of gray hair? Surprised?
They're not the first tribe
to be wiped out.

2.13 Barren and parched
stretches their empty domain—

all our goods plundered, our hopes
false, our camels held
for our children, our spoils robbed
from us by war. The absent
may return but no one makes
it back from death. Is the barren
woman like the mother who's given
birth? Is the raider's loot
like the empty hands of the loser?
No sense asking men for help.
Only God can help—all good
comes from Him. Some requests
are too demanding, like overloading a camel,
but who responds like God? He knows
what men's hearts conceal.
No matter how hard you strive, success
often stems from weakness
and ambition often comes to naught.
Heed Fate, not men. To beseech
them for help is futile—rely
on the dictates of your heart.
Many friends become foes! Come
to the aid of the land you now inhabit.
Pleading you're a stranger is no excuse.
Cut off from our closest kin,
we often create ties with distant
tribes. Life invites
deception and long life
is an agony.

I've drunk from fetid 2.27
pools, their banks strewn
with pin-tailed grouse feathers,
my heart pounding in fear,
on a barren trek of terror,

full of dread at dawn,
my only comrade a speedy
camel, hard as an onager,
her back welded tight,
her withers like a mighty dune,
in her ninth year, a mother
neither old nor young, more like
a dark-coated male ʿĀnāt
onager with scars on his sides,
or an oryx grazing on *rukhāmā*,
battered by the north wind.

2.34 It was like the epic days of yore
when I'd ride this long-stride
barrel-chested mare,
her frame strong, her forelocks
parted by her muzzle, her leg
veins calm, as smooth
as oil, like that mighty hunter
the eagle, her aerie strewn
with bird hearts, fasting
the night through on a lofty cairn,
as rigid, as motionless as an old
woman grieving, the cold
dawn's rime dripping
from her plumes. On the far side
of a barren plain, she spots
a fox, rustles her wings,
and wheels—the first step
to flight. Sensing her, the fox
raises his tail in fear,
a true sign of terror.
As she launches into flight, she picks
up speed like a flash flood

and, shrinking back in panic,
his eyes roll white.
Thwack!—she pounces on her prey,
who falters. Thrown hard
to the ground, the fox's face
is torn by the sharp rocks.
Talons in his sides, again and again
she picks him up and slams him down.
He yelps in pain, but no escape—
her beak drills into his chest.

3

ʿAbīd ibn al-Abraṣ: The Seas of Poetry

3.1 Awake, I watched the lightning, pearl-
bright, rake across mountains
of clouds choked on rain, black,
heavy, like camels in calf, laden
with burdens of water, rain pouring
from their rifts, pitch dark. The earth
thrummed, pelted by drops gouging
the ground like the pits dug by pin-tailed
grouse for their eggs. The clouds mass,
release their flood, racing here and there
like onagers on the run, billowing like ocean
waves, black as deepest night—
when lightning crackles through the gloom,
the stars break out in smiles, like bright-
eyed girls in all their sparkle.

3.8 Ask
the poets—can any swim the seas
of poetry like me or dive as deep
for its pearls? My tongue plunges deeper
for rhyme and line and poem than the fish,
master of the seas, who darts back
and forth in glints of eggshell white,
while other fish, daughters of the deep, swim

warily among the slimy rocks.
Try holding him tight in your hands
and he'll fight hard, squirming to be free,
slippery in his escape. This sea monster
is supple, dark as the waves, clad
in serried scales of burnished mail.

I swear—in time of famine I protect 3.17
my name by feeding the tribe. My father
I revere, my honor I shield, so do not count
me among the greedy, unlike the sponger
who swoops quicker than an eagle on a man's
rations, who besieges a lord's door,
refusing to budge, annoying the guard
who, ready to beat him or grapple
him to the ground, shouts out, "When will we ever
be rid of this cur?"
Were I to value food 3.23
over honor, what could protect
me from scorn? If, driven by hunger,
I should pounce on a share of food,
I'd pray to God, "Please, make me lame!
Please, let my guts writhe in pain!"

4

Al-Muraqqish al-Akbar: When Vultures Enter the Tents

4.1 Are the ruins mute? Why don't they reply?
They'd talk if they could. Once this was Asmā''s
home—it's desolate now, its traces like calligraphy
on a sheet of vellum, a wilderness, overgrown
with blossoms moist with dew. My eyes
stream with tears—she ruined my heart.
The litters left early that morning, as tall
as Malham's palm trees; a scent of musk
wafted on the air, and the women's faces
were as bright as dinars, their fingertips dyed
'anam red.

4.7 How can I be consoled for Fate's
attack? The corpse of my comrade Tha'lab,
helmet splitter and chief in the dark war
days, lies unburied in Taghlam.
Farewell, cousin! I'd give my life for you!
Only the peaks of Shābah and Adam are eternal.

4.10 If anything could escape Fate, the bearded,
white-striped ibex on 'Amāyah ridge
or Mount Khiyam could. He almost touches the sky,
higher than an aerie, on the slopes of a mighty
broad-backed peak where he ranges at will.

Had Death overlooked him, he'd have grown old—
but Fate struck and he slipped and fell to his death.
Who regrets a long life? We all know what the future
holds. Fathers die and are succeeded by sons;
sons become orphans. Mothers get some reward
but then suffer just as acutely as barren women do.

We are not to be blamed for the raid 4.18
by a king of Jafnah, hell-bent on conquest.
We did not commit this outrage! He was a hard,
ruthless warrior with a peerless pedigree
traced back to the saffron-dyed
princesses and uncircumcised men. A rabble
answered his war cry—paupers with no livestock
worth raiding, pale, bareheaded,
not known for acts of generosity. The king
stooped like a saker, like a speckled viper
sloughing its skin, at the head of a vast
army, as dense as Shurayf's trees,
ravaging the land in a riot of rage.

We are your mother's kin—we have the right 4.24
to expect respect and protection. We are not
like those tribes who thrive on shame and violate
rights, useless when prosperous, despicable
in famine years when you see vultures enter
the tents to share a family's meal,
when, from holes in the tent, the smoke drifts
yellow-black like a nag's coat.
When the land bursts into bloom and the meadows
are a tangle of blossoms, the taste of bitter
regret fills their mouths—they'd sooner eat
wild gourds. As a clan, we are driven
by generosity and self-restraint; we use what we own

to protect our souls from any stain of dishonor.
May God always give us the strength to arm
ourselves for the fray and to carry out raids
when the warriors shout, "Camels!" and armies
charge and clamor as night falls. Even youth
knows the taste of ruin—do not hold
a grudge against the old and the wise.

5

Al-Shanfarā: Like a Spleen-Dark Wolf

Up with your camels, brothers! I'm eager to raid 5.1
our foes. The moon is high, we have what we need;
our mounts are saddled, ready for victory. The earth
shelters those who shun hatred and protects the noble
from harm, but a hero on a night raid in quest of spoils
or a mountain retreat should be bold! If you decide
not to raid, I'll turn to other folk who don't reveal secrets
or betray the transgressor for his deeds—the far-ranging wolf,
the speckled viper, the shaggy-maned hyena. These are my kin,
proud and ferocious, but when I sight quarry
I'm no less ferocious! When hands grab for food, I hang back,
for hurry is a sign of greed—my superiority lies
in my noble displays of largesse. I can boast of three
comrades—a bold heart, a burnished blade,
a yellow twanging long-necked smooth-backed bow
trimmed with leather thongs and carried with a strap;
when it fires an arrow, it wails like a woman screaming
for a dead child—what need of those who won't repay a good
deed, whose kinship brings no solace? I'm no feckless drover
who only takes his herd out in the evenings, feeding his young
camels poorly though they could be free to suckle.
I'm no feeble coward who stays at home with his wife,

forever seeking her advice on what to do. I'm no skittish
ostrich, no chick weak on its legs, its heart
fluttering as if borne up and downward by a lark.
I'm no fop, no ladies' man sauntering about the house with hair
slicked back and kohled eyes. I'm no wretched
louse, good for nothing, tongue-tied, weaponless,
easily scared. I never lose my way in the dark,
even if my fleet camel gets confused by the vast trackless
desert, her feet pounding the flinty ground,
causing sparks to fly. I'd rather starve than owe
anything in return, I'd rather eat dirt than have anyone think
I'm beholden to him for his charity. Food and drink
would be mine aplenty but for my refusal of shame,
which my bitter soul won't abide. I must roam
free, twisting my guts against hunger as tightly
as a craftsman deftly twines the strands of a rope.

5.26 Despite my meager fare, I cross the dark
to hunt, like the ravenous lean-hipped spleen-dark wolf
of the wastes who lopes along sideways against the wind,
sniffing for prey as he speeds through the tail ends of ravines.
Carrion diverts him from his course, his call answered
by other grizzled scrawny wolves, lank as the clack
of arrows in a gambler's hands or an angry swarm
of bees, their hive stirred by the sticks of a honey gatherer
high on the rock face. Their mouths agape, their jaws
as thin as splintered branches, the wolves grimace,
emitting a chorus of howls on the plain like the keens
of women wailing on a hilltop. Finding comfort
in shared misery, the pack blinks and howls at each other.
Their laments now exchanged, now assuaged—
what good are empty laments?—they turn away
and retrace their paths, picking up speed, putting
a brave face on their inner disarray.

The dust-colored 5.36
sandgrouse drink from the pond I leave behind,
their curved wings beating after a night's journey
toward water. Our goal was the same, so we began
to race—they flew hard, but proved no match
for my speed. I left the pond as they dove in, their necks
and stomachs drenched, their racket as loud as droves
of camels descending on a well and jostling for water
to slake their thirst. The sandgrouse drank in hasty
gulps, then sped away again like dawn raiders
fleeing from Uḥāẓah.

At night when I lie down, I greet 5.42
the ground with a painful humpback of raw vertebrae,
my emaciated joints knuckled like the bone dice tossed
by gamers. If War, the mother of battle murk, is angry
with Shanfarā, I've long been her pride and joy, exiled
for crimes that cast lots for my flesh, my carcass
fated for whichever one wins the prize. I doze
but they sleep with open eyes, hastening to destroy me.
I'm wracked with cares that assail me time and again,
grimmer than a quartan fever—I repel them but they return,
attacking me from high and low.

You may see me in the midday 5.49
sun like the daughter of the dunes, walking barefoot
in penury, but I'm clad in the armor of fortitude, with the heart
of a *simʿ*—instead of sandals I wear resolve. Now rich, now poor—
riches come to the man resolved to risk
all he owns!—I make no show of the misery of poverty
or the jubilant swagger of the wealthy, my judgment is not shaken
by extreme acts, I am deaf to the idle gossip
that fuels malicious slander!

On an ill-starred, bitter 5.54
night when the hunter burns his bow and arrow shafts
to keep warm, I went out into the gloom and the rain—

my only comrades in arms were hunger, fear, and the wintry
cold. I went to widow wives and orphan
children before coming back in the black of night.
The next day in Ghumayṣā’, people sat around the campfire,
one group asking questions, the others silent:
"Our dogs growled last night, and we wondered:
was it a wolf or a young hyena on the prowl?
The dogs soon went back to sleep, so we thought:
was a grouse or falcon spooked? If a jinni did this,
it paid us a dire visit; if it was a human—impossible!"

5.61 Dog days when the mirage melts and flows like water,
when the ground's too hot for vipers, I'm out there
with no cloth or scarf to protect me, clad in my tattered
atḥamī robe, my hair a thick, tangled
mass of uncombed knots blown by the wind,
a stranger to the touch of oil or delousing, matted
into clumps of filth, unwashed for ages.

5.65 A desert
waste flat as the back of a shield, rough
to traverse. From one end to the other I cross it on foot,
then climb a peak where I watch, on the lookout,
as the ibex crowd around me like maidens in fringed
gowns circling an idol. At night they sleep
beside me as if I were a white-leg long-horn buck
scaling the steep scarps to my mountain retreat.

6

Ṣakhr al-Ghayy: The Workings of Fate

Death has laid Abū ʿAmr on the highlands beneath a heap of stones— 6.1
a life gone! With her snares she lured a desert viper from its nest.
Death has defeated my last brother's charms and amulets.

Why weep? Fate hunts the full-grown ibex in his glade 6.4
under wisps of clouds unwound like turbans. He enjoys
a long life of ease in his mountain home, the points of his ridged
horns like fingertips. At the sight of night's approach, he sleeps
in his covert, an old man wrapped in a cloak, estranged from
his folk,
complaining of harsh treatment by his sons, with no hope of
redress.
Tangles of fragrant *bashām* leaves, like loosened locks,
dangle in front of him, in the slopes where he was born and grew
to adulthood, surrounded by mighty mature rams. Spooked
by a crow's caw, fleet and nimble, he springs across the rocks.
One day, after many years of life, Fate confronts him
with the youngest son of a shaykh bent with age and starving,
who shelters his father in winter and zealously forages fruit
for him in summer, like a man pleading his case before a judge.
He spots the ibex and exclaims, "By God! Who's seen a white-
leg as big as this in our day? He'll keep our father
alive until the stars bring the rains." He stalks him

and at close range fires a hard arrow with a cleft head,
true to its aim. Shouting to his brother, he closes in with a knife
and briskly butchers the ibex.

6.17 Fate hunts the majestic
supple-winged eagle who rests her two fledglings on a bed
of hare flesh, the hearts of birds stored inside her nest like date
pits discarded by a reveler. She swoops down on a fawn
she'd spotted lying by acacias, neglected by its idmi mother.
As she passes a ledge she damages her wing and in great pain
lands on her feet in the barrens. When she flaps her wing
in the air it sounds like the twisted rags used in games of mock
fighting. Her eaglets, left in the nest with no food or protection,
are terrified at dawn by a crow's caw or the wind's sough.
After that night they never see her again and know no rest,
calling to one another without end.

6.24 Such are the workings of Fate—
master of both hunter and fleet-footed prey.

7

Labīd ibn Rabīʿah: In the Grip of the North Wind

Minā, Ghawl, and Rijām are a wilderness, 7.1
the tribe's dwelling places in ruin,
Rayyān's watercourses stripped bare,
faint as writing scratched on rock.
Gone too are the dunghills. So many years
of war and peace have passed since I knew her
who walked there. Spring's stars have brought
heavy rain and drizzle from dawn showers
and storms from cloud banks that come
at night in a chorus of thunderclaps.
The *ayhuqān* is tall; gazelles and ostriches
rear their young on the wadi's slopes;
the oryx rest with their calves, safe
in herds on the open plain. Uncovered
by the spring torrents, the ruins were like faded
words written on a monk's psalter
or indigo circles painted by a tattoo
artist. I had so many questions—
but why interrogate such mute immortal
rocks? Here the tribe once lived
and now it's empty: only panic grass and the trench
remain. You wept that morning when the women
took shelter in their creaking howdahs,

shaded by silk brocade behind patterned
red curtains. Like Tūḍiḥ's oryx
and Wajrah's does tending to their fawns,
they left in groups, screened by veils
of heat haze, like the mighty rocks and tamarisks
on Bīshah's slopes. But why remember Nawār
of Murrah? She's far away and all our bonds
are broken. She's settled in Fayd, next to Hijaz,
on the Twin Mountains' eastern slopes;
or in Muḥajjar, secure in Fardah and Rukhām;
or, if she made for Yemen, she's in Ṣuwā'iq,
in Ṭulkhām, or by Qahr's black boulders.
What hopes can I have of her? Our ties are cut—
I need her no more. The best comrade
is the one who cuts friendship's bonds. Be noble
to those who claim to wish you well—break
with them for good if they betray you with lies.

7.22 I must prove my worth on a hardy camel
whose loin and hump have grown so lean
from frequent desert crossings that her bones
stick out, her fur is patchy, and her leg
straps frayed, yet she's still nimble in the reins,
swift as reddish clouds emptied of rain
driven hard by the south wind,
or as an onager in foal switching her tail,
the mate of a white-bellied jack
battered by his rivals' kicks and nips,
his hide pocked with bites, who, worried
by her resistance, drives her over the hills
across Thalabūt's rugged tracts,
where he stands on a peak like a sentry
watching the land. Six months into the year,
at Jumada's end, when their hooves trod

on prickly awns and the simoom blasted
the air, they had grazed enough, without a drink
of water for ages, so they resolved to be on the move—
hard work ensures success! They raced,
kicking up a tall pillar of dust,
plumes flitting like smoke from a fire
fanned by the north wind and kindled
with *ʿarfaj* twigs into an explosion of flames.
The jack kept her in front: if she swerved
from the path, he'd push her back into the lead.
They came to a deep pond whose water
fed some palm trees, where the *qullām* grew
thick, surrounded by reeds, shaded
by tangles of thickets.
Or is my camel like an oryx, 7.36
a snub-nose doe left behind
by the herd, roaming the wadis in search
of her lost young, its white corpse
lying in the dust devoured by gray
wolves, who, expert hunters, snatched
her calf—Fate's arrows never miss.
That night, exposed to showers that soaked
the trees, she hid under scraggly roots
at the base of shifting sands, far
from the beaten track, her back exposed
to the rain on a night when the stars were hidden
by thick banks of cloud, shining
in the gloom as bright as a pearl fallen
from a snapped necklace. At first light, she emerged
out of the dark, hooves slipping on wet
ground, darting in panicked circles
over Ṣuʿāʾid's slopes for seven long
nights and days; she began to despair
when her teats shrank with no calf to suckle.

Suddenly she was on the alert—a faint noise
of men, her mortal foes, its source
hidden. Where did the sound come from?
From the front, she thought; then—no, from the rear.
The hunters knew their arrows were useless
and sicced their tightly collared, drop-eared
dogs trained to kill. She attacked
them with horns like iron hairpins, sharp-
edged and battle-hard as Samharī spears—
she knew that Fate would bring her death
if she couldn't drive them away. After a lunge,
Wolfie lay drenched in blood, Blackie
dead. Beyond reproach, this is how I conquer
the desert wastes when the horizon blinds
and dances at midday, the hills clad
in robes of heat haze.
7.57 Nawār, did you fail
to realize that it is I who ties and severs
bonds, who shuns places I find unpleasant,
unless they be where Death will trap my soul?
You know nothing of the nights of drink
and cheer I've enjoyed, of the merchant's stalls
I've visited when wine was sold at a premium,
paying the full price for black wineskins
and ancient pitch-smeared jars
opened and poured into cups,
morning drinks of a choice wine,
to the sound of the strings of a lute strummed
exquisitely by a singer—while folk slept,
I raced to beat cockcrow and gulp
my second drink. You know nothing
of how I've sheltered the poor on a bitter-
cold day in the grip of the north wind;

of the cover I've offered the raiders,
fully armored on my spirited warhorse,
charging with her reins tied around my body;
of how I've kept guard in dangerous frontiers
where the battle murk rises to the cairns on the hilltops;
of how at night when the sun yielded
to the gloom I've rejoined our troops, our camp
secure, mounted on a mare whose neck
is like the mighty trunk of a palm tree
stripped of leaves, its dates too high
for farmers to harvest; of how we've sped faster
than the ostrich, my horse's light frame
on fire, her saddle creaking, her breast
soaked in sweat, her girth covered
in foam, lunging and rising in her reins,
sprinting as fast as a sandgrouse racing
waterward over hard ground. You know
nothing of how at gatherings full of strangers,
where men fear shame, and victory
can be won, where strong-necked warriors,
feet planted square like desert jinn,
threaten dire retaliation, I've defeated
imposters and asserted our demands for my tribe's
bloodwite, my proud words an easy
match for the nobles; of how I've made barren camels
and camels in calf the prize in a *maysir*
contest played with unmarked arrows,
lavishing the meat on those we protect—
our guests and wards think they've entered
the fertile, verdant vale of Tabālah.
Women dressed in rags, weakened
by disease like camels left to die
at their master's grave, flock to my tent,

where, as the winds contend, the orphans come
to feast from my cauldrons swollen high
with rivers of meat.

7.78 At tribal gatherings,
we respond resolutely to times of famine,
giving each clan its share of plunder—
sometimes more, for generosity is our way, open-
handed with the spoils of war, proud
leaders of our people, following a code
fixed by our ancestors—all peoples follow
the example set by their founders. In the dread
of combat, armed with spears, we fasten
helmets over our chain mail, iron hauberks
untarnished by the rust of shame, as bright
as stars in the sky, heroes who never flinch
or indulge a whim, heirs of an illustrious
past to which young and old aspire!
The Lord has given each tribe its character,
so be content with your lot! To us He has given
fidelity. When disaster strikes, we set to work
as arbiters or knights, showering gifts
as welcome as the spring rain on the neighbors
under our care and on the women in their first
year of widowhood. Who can cast an evil
eye upon us? What foe can impugn our honor?

8

Al-Muzarrid ibn Ḍirār: My Flood of Words

My heart recovered and my critics relented, 8.1
but I struggled to give up my love for Salmā—
it lasted through all my youthful follies
until my head became a shock of gray
dyed with henna, its roots white
like *thaghāmah* tips—gray hair
is a grim sign that Death's at the door.
Youth's vigor was my gracious companion
in those reckless days when I so delighted
in Salmā's small talk, ever receptive
to my desires, eggshell smooth, seductive,
a marvel to the pleasure-seeker's eyes,
nights when she'd dally around me,
bewitching all with her languid steps,
her doe eyes like an oryx in a herd grazing
on juicy, rain-soaked grasses,
her black hair lush, its tresses
like Rammān's willowy black snakes,
her legs like papyrus stalks swaying
in a pond fed by gurgling springs.

When War bares her fangs, fame 8.12
is only won by arms. Dhubyān warriors
know well that I'm the knight who battles

for his own kind, that I ram the champion
with repeated thrusts of my bloodied lance,
its thirst never slaked, that when War gives
birth and disaster looms, I ride forth
on my steed, the length of his back gathered
into his withers, always first to the post,
perfect in his lines, generous with every gallop,
descended from Ṣarīḥ, neighing like a shrill
chorus of fifes and timbrels at a feast,
with a goshawk's glare when ridden and measured
steps when led by the halter. "Is he a tent
on a hilltop or a wolf at his lookout?" you ask,
seeing him standing there stock-still.
He outstrips all other chargers, ensuring your safety—
the mark of a true thoroughbred—as he speeds you
toward your target, and, in the chase, startles
the onagers, felling them like a troop of camels
slaughtered by some feckless show-off. He stares,
eyes bulging as if sensing fear,
ears cocked, ever alert after a hard
run, while other horses' eyes sink
deep like empty rock pools.
I push him hard till his ribcage resembles
a woven mat with wide gaps
between its fronds of palm. He runs
as if bolting and cantering were a vow he had
to fulfill, his flanks and loins fused,
his ribs a row of curves so bare
of flesh they're like arrows pared by a master
craftsman, his hooves so hard he has no care
if he's racing over rocks or hillocks of sand.

8.28 My other mount's a short-haired, long-backed
mare of great power and endurance,

a roan, barren, as hard as a mighty
staff, her back large-framed, her pedigree
traced back to Ṣarīḥ and Jāfil. She loves
stretching out into a gallop, high-strung, tireless—
she adores deserts without end. After a long
run her cheeks twitch like an angry
man flapping his hands before a judge.
Her noble resolve and practiced pace
give her the lead in the charge. In a free
rein, she veers like a grouse fleeing
the swoop of a saker in yarak. We keep
her close to our tent, only saddling her for raids—
she'll never foal. She's in her prime,
like a fawn fed on *ḥullab*, her upper body
torqued, her lower flanks firmly knotted.
A prize possession—long owned and cherished!
I'll never part with her as long as oil
is pressed, as long as men, rich and poor,
walk this earth.
I'm clad in a body- 8.38
length Tubbaʿ coat of mail
that ripples like spilled water, with tightly
nailed rings, smooth as the scales
of a huge fish, proof against broad
arrowheads, spears, and piercing darts.
Burnished and brightly striped, its mesh
tightly serried, it reaches past
my fingertips. When tribes are mustered
for battle and lives are at stake, all the soldiers
celebrate its fame. I wear a neck
guard fitted to a smooth, round
Ḥimyarite helmet to protect me from rocks—
in the sun it blazes like the candles in a monk's
lamp. I bear a shield as bright as the sun

in the dark of night. I wield a keen blade
of pure iron that cuts through anything it touches,
its edge never blunted, forged
by our ancestors, as well as a smooth Indian
sword that slices through armor
well into the shoulders. Rushing into the fray,
the warrior cries, "You're the best of blades,
pure, too sharp for the helms, keen,
never dulled no matter how many blows
you strike!" Unsheathed, the blade soughs,
polished bright by the smiths. And I carry
a straight spear whose smooth nodes
and solid haft are as if covered in a film
of oil. It's fitted with a well-honed head,
tapered like a new moon on a pitch-
black night. When brandished, it quivers
like a snake slithering over sand dunes.

8.53 What do you think of the dire threats
I've received from fools who attack my honor
behind my back? These men are pitiful, mere puppies,
not men enough to sully my honor!
I'm strong, battle-hardened—my foes whimper
in fear. For forty years my blows
have been true! My fame as orator and marksman
is familiar from days of old. I attack
with my immortal poems sung everywhere
by night travelers and caravan guides.
Easy to memorize, they pass from mouth
to mouth, resounding throughout the land,
growing ever brighter when repeated by lips
that keenly test the worth of poetry.
My poems assault my foes, leaving
on their faces an indelible stain like a mole.

This is how the trade in invective ends—
my flood of words never runs dry,
the sound of my voice never grates.

Great poets can craft any theme 8.63
into verse! Turn your skills to portray
a poverty-stricken Ṣubāḥī hunter
who owns but a few *raqam* arrows of his own device,
a hard yellow bow, and a litter
of dogs whose collars rattle on their necks—
Blackie, Tipcat, Beanpole, Shorthair,
Wolfie, and Fetch—daughters of a pair
of salukis, his life and soul before their death.
He knew this meant starvation and failure—
his fame and fortune vanished. His daemon
reminded him he had a family to feed,
so he made the rounds, asking his friends
to repay his gifts, but all his entreaties went
unanswered. He returned to his arrow-thin boys
and foolish wife who wasted all her days
with the neighbors—such wives are the very worst!
"Anything to eat?" he asked. "Damn
your brothers! I curse mankind." "Yes, the water
in the well," she replied, "and that charred sliver
of shriveled skin we've had on hand for a year."
He lost his appetite. Exhausted, with no prospect
of relief, he lay huddled in his cloak,
but his worries kept him from sleep.

9

Abū Dhu'ayb: Fate the Hunter

9.1 Has Fate, no friend of grief, shocked
you into tears? What's wrong with your body,
despite your riches? Why is every bed
you lie on a bed of stones? asked
Umaymah. My sons are dead, I said.
Their death has caused me so much pain.
Since they bade me farewell, I sigh
and cry and cannot sleep. I used to think
weeping was a folly, but loss forces us
to tears. In their haste they ignored my advice;
now they're gone forever! True, all must sleep
the sleep of death; yet, though I know I'll join
them soon, I'm left behind to live
a life of agony. I tried hard to protect
them, but who can stop Death? What use
are charms when Death grips you in its claws?
I cry myself blind, my eyes burning
as if pierced with thorns; I'm a stone weathered
by Time in Musharraq's shrine. Fate
hasn't humbled me—I put on a brave face
for foes who would rejoice in my pain.
Train the soul to be happy with less—
the more you indulge it, the more it craves.

Who can flee Fate the Hunter? 9.15
Not the onager with his harem of four mares,
braying like a slave attacked by wolves.
Well fed on grass, he drinks from the pools
on the plains watered by frequent cloudbursts,
a jenny, slender as a spear, by his side.
As his harem tarried, butting heads,
he grew grave, then frisky, but his luck ran
out: the pools dried, and he sealed
his fate by driving his mares to water.
From Sawā' to Bathr, he risked the open
road. On the slopes between Nubāyiʿ
and Dhū l-ʿArjā', the jennies were like a herd of camels
rounded up in a raid or a clutch of arrows
scattered in a gambler's game, as he drove
them hard, like a smith whetting a blade.
When bright Canopus hunkered over Orion
like a gambler, the troop waded leg-
deep onto the pebbles of a cold pond.
They drank, then heard a noise on the far side
of a hill—like a thud or the rasp of a bow
held by a hunter poised for the kill.
The herd shied behind the barrel-chested
jack and a lean jenny. Then the hunter
shot a mare in foal—the arrow
lay on the ground in a pool of blood.
As the jack turned and exposed his flank,
the hunter groped in his quiver and a swift
Ṣāʿidī shaft struck the beast
deep in his ribs. Death was dealt
by the hunter—a few mares bolted,
barely alive; others fell to their knees,
slipping in the gore, their legs as if
wrapped in striped Tazīdī cloaks.

9.36 Who can flee Fate the Hunter?
Not the scared oryx buck, spooked
by the hunting dogs at dawn, sheltered
by the roots of the *arṭā* from the howling wind
and rain, peering into the dark to discover
the source of the sound. As daylight warms
his back, the first dogs appear
at the head of the dusky pack and he panics.
Darting out, his path blocked by the hounds,
he charges, his sharp horns dyed
red, while his muscled limbs and striped
flanks keep their jaws at bay.
The dogs retreat as he lunges at the yelping
pack, wielding his horns like skewers
of bloody meat served at a feast.
With his slender-tipped, short-fletched
arrows in his hand, the hunter advances
and fires, allowing his dogs to escape—
the dart drives deep into the oryx's
flank as he falls to the ground with a crash,
more majestic than a prized bull camel.

9.49 Who can flee Fate the Hunter?
Not the helmeted, ironclad warrior
whose face is covered in rust and sweat
from the heat of his chain mail, mounted
on a sunken-eyed mare grown fat
on milk into whose flesh his fingers sink.
Un-foaled, with empty teats like earrings,
she snaps the saddle ring with her pace,
but even when whipped, lathered in sweat,
thigh veins bulging, she keeps
her best speed in reserve. One day
as he feints and parries, Fate brings

him face to face with a champion mounted
on a light-framed colt as nimble
as a sure-footed ibex. The heroes dismount
and fight for glory's prize, their warhorses
staring each other down. Both fighters
are proud of their skills—but it's an evil day!
They're armed with keen, fine-tempered
blades that hack off limbs, and Yazan
spears whose heads gleam like lamps,
clad in full-length, honey-smooth hauberks
forged by David or Tubbaʿ—both lie dead
from wounds like rips in cloth beyond repair.
They lived for glory and fame—but why?

10

Al-Ḥuṭay'ah: Slaughter Me, Father

10.1 Without food for three nights,
he hugged his empty stomach,
as dry as sand, in the unpeopled
wastes. Wild, uncouth,
a stranger to human company,
as rough as a thorn tree,
he deemed desert hardships
a life of blessed ease.
He lived in a lonely gully
with his crone, who lurked behind
three strange creatures
you'd think were wild animals:
they were barefoot, naked,
and had never once tasted
baked bread. Out of the gloom
a figure loomed—a guest!
In panic, the man jumped
to his feet. His son noticed
his distress and said, "Slaughter
me, Father, and give him his full
portion of meat! Don't plead
poverty as an excuse: our visitor

may think we are rich in cattle
  and cover our name with shame."
He considered this plan but shrank
  in fear—he had almost sacrificed
his son. "O Lord!" he prayed.
  "We've nothing to feed our guest.
By all that is good, please
  don't deprive him of meat tonight."

A herd of onagers appeared 10.10
  in the distance, trotting in file
behind the jack, thirsty,
  headed for water. He crept
after them: his need was greater
  than theirs. He waited till the thirstiest
had drunk their fill, then, plucking
  an arrow from his quiver, he fired—
a jenny fell to the ground,
  the mother of a newborn foal,
in her prime, her rich meat
  stored under layers of fat.
What joy he felt as he dragged
  her back to his family! How they rejoiced
when they saw her bloody wound!
  That night they honored their guest
and feasted like lords. The kill
  had freed them from the grim debt
of spilling their child's blood.
  Elated, the father and mother
welcomed the guest as their son.

11

Ḥumayd al-Arqaṭ: A Tall-Necked Horse

11.1 Night's cloak is tasseled with red
as dawn herds away the gloom
and its retinue of sparkling stars.
I sit astride a long-necked horse,
pliant in rein, swift of charge,
leaving the other steeds behind
as it sprints in the lead of a race,
11.10 like a canny, hook-beak gos
shaking the rime and rain from her
feathers, ruthless in pursuit
of her quarry. In terror, the birds
fly to the trees, trying
to escape a gaze unwavering
in its reach—her eyes embedded
in a rocklike head, she senses
motion from afar—a hunter
whose lids have never been seeled.

12

Ghaylān ibn Ḥurayth: A Hunter since Her Youth

The night still concealed 12.1
by its hijab, I carry a molted
gos, a hunter since her youth.
When she strikes with her curved talons,
her screech is like the scream
of a battle-frenzied warrior;
her attack, when cast, like a stone; 12.6
her beak thrusts like a short
spear. Pitiless to houbaras,
hearts ripped from breasts.
Impaled on the furrier's knives
or butcher's hooks of her talons,
they writhe and jump, faces
ground into the dirt as she stabs
deeper and deeper into their flesh.

13

Ghaylān ibn Ḥurayth: A Stipple-Cheeked Gos

13.1 Night was worn out—
I roused a good-natured
falconer, neat in his tunic,
still groggy from strong drafts
of sleep during night's duel
with day. He promptly rose
and fetched a stipple-cheeked
gos, in yarak, legs
bare, an angry brute.
In two casts, she hunted
twenty-five, then fifteen.
Look! So many houbaras
lying in the dust, pierced
by her talons and beak. Feted
at the hunt's end, she sat
tall and you'd think her keel
had been dyed saffron or ochre
from the gore spilled from guts.
She indulged her desires—hearts
and chunks of juicy flesh.

14

Al-Shamardal ibn Sharīk: Her Assegai Beak

Night lingered on as day 14.1
flickered beneath her hijab,
a mix of dark and light.
Through the gloom I carried
a Tawwajī gos, trained
from youth, never failing
to fly back to her handler,
obstinate once, now pliant,
recognizing all the signals.
As he readied her before the sun
unleashed the mirages, I cried,
"With sight this keen, she can spot
quarry in the upper reaches
of Malḥūb from her perch—on the wing
she could even see Tibet!" Hitting
her prey like a stone, she scattered
her spoils in the dust or undergrowth—
such fury!—hares yelping
as her assegai beak wreaked
havoc, expertly tearing
hearts from breasts, talons
sunk deep into their hides,

like butcher's cleavers or skewers,
her gorge dyed saffron
or dark with slaughterhouse blood,
or ringed with a choker of scented
musk. She tallied up eighty
kills of houbara and hare,
strung up for the guests invited
on the hunt, their campfire a feast
of birds roasted and grilled,
prepared by a handsome youth
who welcomed our honeyed words.

15

Al-Shamardal ibn Sharīk: His Dark Elation

As my comrades dozed off, 15.1
talking late into the night,
I taught the wolf a lesson
when he put me to the test.
I saw my sheep bolting off
and, barely dressed, drowsily
got to my feet. Thrilled
with his kill, he loped away
in his dark elation, like a pillar
of dust kicked up by the wind.
Several times I chased him
away and several times
he came back. Then I knew
I had no choice—my flock
would be wiped out. He lunged
at my hand and my heart missed
a beat. I steadied myself
and fired an arrow—with a limp
he slinked away. That night,
safe and sound, I exulted,
"God be praised!"

16

Al-Shamardal ibn Sharīk: An Irate Stare

16.1 Just before sunrise
I cross the dark,
hoping for a lucky day
with a curve-beaked gos
clad in chain mail, last
fed yesterday, hungrily
scanning the pond at Ṭams
and beyond with an irate stare
or the eyes of a man in fever's
grip. When cast, she spots
twenty dusty houbaras,
waddling like women, backs
bent with bundles of firewood,
or like Christians in dark robes.
The houbaras lay scattered
in groups of four and five,
brains oozing from their skulls,
her talons as if steeped in *wars*
from guts ripped open,
with one of the males humbled
in death, his head twisted
like a camel responding to a tug
on the rope. The gos stares

at the left hand of her skilled
handler and stands tall
as a rock, a smooth stone
fired from a trebuchet's sling.

17

Al-Shamardal ibn Sharīk: A Dark Gos

17.1 A dark Tawwajī gos
of pure descent, firmly
perched on my left hand

18

Al-Shamardal ibn Sharīk: Like a Mill

Like a mill, she grinds 18.1
leverets into the ground,
her irate beak
tearing at their faces

19

Al-Shamardal ibn Sharīk: Clothes Ignite

19.1 Dawn yelled,
driving night
away, peering
out from her hijab
and lifting the hem
of her jilbab, like a steed
with piebald flanks,
or a torch carried
by a man running
to light a fire—
the flames leap
in the wind and his clothes
ignite in a blaze

20

Al-Shamardal ibn Sharīk: Like Two Rubies

Her eyes shining bright 20.1
like two precious rubies

21

Al-Shamardal ibn Sharīk: Dawn Shines Pink

21.1 Early, when the pink
of dawn glows
in the dark,
I go hunting

22

Abū l-Najm al-ʿIjlī: Harried by the Jinn

A deserted water hole ruined 22.1
by time—its waterskins lay unused
and only the tribe's hearth
and ashes could be recognized.
I pulled on the reins of my camel
under the cloak of night.

High above the uplands, the storm 22.6
cloud brooded, the birds
fleeing its gloom; rain
battered the earth and the water
soon flooded the hills, the debris
strewn like flour on a dark robe,
sweeping the *shīḥ* shrubs
into the *ṭaḥmāʾ*. The water hole filled
up again and, like a dog returning
to its vomit, its generosity resumed.
Like a man coming home
to his wives, the water spilled
over into the trough where it rose
and washed away the mounds
of earth clogging up its edges.
Faster than the blink of an eye

it burst, flooding the salt flats
and the *ṭarfāʾ* trees on the slopes,
then flowed to a remote wilderness
where no one had foraged for truffles,
and the rocks were transformed into a field
of blossoms, a riot of buds
in sunburst flames decked
with yellow roses; like a singer's
trill, the long, drawn-out screech
of a hopper in the *darmāʾ* grass
answered the chirruping larks.

22.31 An ostrich lifted its neck
like a banner or a bargeman's pole
raised high over the other boatmen;
with a shake of its tentlike wings
clenched together as tightly
as a miser's fist, the ostrich ran
as fast as a well bucket
slipping from the water carrier's
grasp when the rope snaps.
He had been without water for days.
He raised the eyes in his bald
head and approached the trough,
where, all caution gone,
his yellow lips drank—
the first draft cured
the staggers that had made him shake
like a halfwit. As he stood
high on an outcrop, his feathers
22.46 looked like a splash of color
on a dark gown, rustling
like the wind in the gaps of a reed

shelter as he raced over plains
and slopes, leaving a rainbow
of hill flowers in his wake,
running so fast his flesh
was disjoined from his sinews—
other than his belly, where white
feathers shone through the dark,
he looked like a hide smeared
with pitch. Harried by the calls
of the twenty jinn who drove
him on, screaming at him
if he swiveled his small-eared head
or tried to escape, he kicked
up a dust cloud, making it hard
for us to keep him in view.
He'd pass the night beside his nest, 22.64
where a mate kept watch
on her eggs, until a chick
hatched and slept nearby,
like a tent tied to its pegs.
Night-blind, unable to feed
in the dark, he foraged all day
for succulent *sala'* and *ḥuwwā'ah*,
digging up the moist soil
and dry earth with his two-
toed feet, and using his beak
to extract red *dhubaḥ*
and sea onion from the slopes,
feasting on *ḥazā'* in the sand
and scree, swallowing stones
and rocks; his long, supple
gullet gulped down *suṭṭāḥ*
and lush *ḥarshā'*, which moved

down his neck in lumps
like a snake coiled in its nest,
finally reaching his guts.

22.81 He startled the birds above
as he tucked his feathers tight
to fly between ground and sky.
The proud-spirited steed,
as big as a building, pulled
on the bit and gave him chase,
sprinting from the dust cloud
like a lunatic undressing or sidelocks
untied from a shaved head.
Blinded by panic, the ostrich
veered to the side: you could make
out the ground between his legs
as he moved like an archer in his tabard
or like a shock of white hair
on a dark collar or like a star
fired at a rebellious devil
tumbling from the sky.

22.95 I cried
to Shaybān, "Closer! Get him!
We'll feast the tribe on meat
before Orion touches the horizon!"
Trousers hoisted to waist,
mounted high on its withers,
the saddle flecked with sweat,
he pushed the horse to the limit
and, with a spear thrust bloodied
with gore, felled the ostrich,
who crashed to the ground like a pack
camel laden with gear.

23

Abū l-Najm al-ʿIjlī: Dyed Dark with Gore

I was about to depart 23.1
when Bujaylah said, "Father,
stay clear of danger."
God, be merciful;
grant her a long life
free from pain and poverty!
My daughter, we all must rest
in the grave one day. When Death
comes and our end is nigh,
it matters little where we are—
we don't hasten our death
by staying at home or leaving:
as the Revelation makes clear,
it is God's decree. Fear
will not bring me back to you.
My sword belt is tied, my turban
wound. Who can interpret the caw
of the crow? Maybe it brings
good news. Go to your mother,
my child, close your eyes and rest—
calamity has made me impervious
to joy. Fate has never allowed
a father to live just because

he has a girl as young as you.
23.10 Once, I was surrounded by my family's
tents—they're gone, but I know
their lineages. I will suffer their fate—
after a brief spell of life,
we all belong to the past.
If I return home, child,
and my plan succeeds, we'll be rich.
If you hear of my death, mourn
a father whose prowess in war
made his enemies cower in fear.
Ask God for forgiveness; don't forget Him.
Do good—God rewards
those who do good. Don't let Satan
tempt you to tear your clothes
and scratch your face. When, weak
and fearing starvation, like a palm
tree stripped of its branches
and leaves by a farmer, I lost
my horses and camels, I made
my resolve known as the second
year of famine ruined us—
let it be the last of its kind!

23.19 I chose a mature Mahrī,
a spirited female of good
breed, pliant, short-haired,
never in calf or milked as a mother,
left by the drover to pasture
alone; like a strong jack
with his harem, telling them when to go
to water and when to leave,
standing on a hilltop braying

and whinnying at shadows, full
of swagger, walking boldly
like a lame camel with a diseased
shoulder, his females fleeing,
yet recognizing him as their leader
from the bite marks on his neck.

Or is my camel like a solitary white, 23.25
black-legged oryx,
walking through the lush grass
after the spring rains? Feeding
in the fields to the screech of insects
and lit up by a flash of lightning,
he looks like a man clad
in white cotton beside a fire.
The rains come down heavy
with thunder booming in the cloud
banks, soaking him through,
a bitter east wind blowing
all night long. Tired and cold
in the wadi's bend, the rain
falling hard, he digs with his hooves,
seeking shelter beneath an *arṭā*
tree on a curve of sand.

The morning sun, enlivened 23.31
by a north wind, shone
in all its glory. The bull bolted
like a pearl-bright star,
startled to see a hungry
hunter desperate for a kill,
with his lean-hipped, drop-
eared dogs in leather

collars. Sicced, they gave
chase, but he was not an easy catch—
through the flatlands
they raced, matching him leap
for leap in the soft marshy
ground, uprooting the *khuzāmā*
flowers torn and scattered
at their feet. Now, despite their effort,
he's in the lead; now they're close.
After two miles, the dogs
were defeated. Had he wished,
he could have fled to safety
but his warrior soul surged
with rage and he wheeled to attack,
thrusting his horns into their ribs
as they scattered around him on the plain.
Dyed dark with gore,
they fought for their lives
drawing their last breath,
flanks dripping with blood.
23.41 Unhurt, free of care,
the bull went his way,
his horns as if dipped in saffron
and tree bark. This is what I compared
my camel to when her handler brought
her on the day of departure, a Mahrī
easy with her pace, submissive
to the saddle, not used for breeding,
and kept away from camels
raised for trade. I nurtured
her till her hump grew too large
for most saddles, so I cinched
a Quṣwān saddle around her girth.
She was keen to race across the desert

flats—we were sixty days from the king's
palace, the wastes presenting
terrors even for the hardened rider.
"My camel, Lord Hishām is our goal!
He will fulfill our petition!"
Neck outstretched, she covered
hard ground and soft,
feet bruised by the rocks.
When the midday sun was at its height
and ill-fated men carried high
on their biers, she entered the lowlands.
When the sparrows rested in their nests,
she maintained her pace, scaring
the gazelle from its covert. At night's
end, as darkness took to flight,
she stopped in sight of a water hole,
speeding past the deserts
and uplands of Falj and Fulayj.
She devoured the roads and defiles
of the wadis she faced, crossing them
though her fodder had dried up
and the strap at the front of her saddle
rocked slackly to and fro.
She only drank when she could rest
beside pools covered in sandgrouse
feathers and down. She traversed
Samāwah at night—even a Yabrīn
jinni would have complained the next day.
Finally, she saw the mountains 23.57
of Syria girt in a heat haze:
when the haze sank, they looked
near—as the haze tried to climb
in the air above the mountain
peaks, it vanished in defeat.

I came close to giving up
when the saddle straps of our troop
of pale-fawn camels slapped
against the ropes tied at their flanks.
We were hunted by a wolf tracking
their bleeding feet. I scared
him off with my sword and he slunk
away. After two months
of thirst, my camel was skin,
bones, and sinews—she didn't even groan
when struck with the whip.

23.63 Sire, my petition is easy
to grant. I'm not a man who indulges
in frivolity. My heart is heavy
at the thought of losing my lands
if you don't grant me the means
to preserve them. In supplication
I stretch out my hand—bless
it with a good and gracious generosity,
raise me from the depths of calamity—
Fate has stripped away the last
of my branches. Our hopes rest
in you, ruler of Arabs and non-Arabs,
glorious king, son
of a king, youthful brother
of kings whose faces glow
with the caliphate, like gold set
in pure silver, who act
as they see fit and justly impose
the penalty for bloodshed
before kin demand vengeance.

24

Abū l-Najm al-ʿIjlī: Full of Bloodlust

Under the spell of lovely girls, 24.1
I prepared my camels for departure.

* *

We halted in the heart of Jumayrāt, 24.3
the best of places, blessed
with oryx and houbara. When it was time
to enjoy the hunt, the huntsman
brought on his obedient cheetahs
perched on the horses' rumps;
on the plain they scowled, eyes
raised, poised and alert,
ready to pounce like fierce
demons, natural-born
killers now trained for the hunt;
what a sight to see them blink
with their bright, flecked eyes,
black lines stretching
down their cheeks, and striped, twitchy
tails like a viper's coils.
We reached the flats, amid the lush 24.20
plants growing in furrows
left by the plow. The cheetahs
raced toward the snub-nosed oryx

grazing in groups, their compact
    paws kicking out sideways
and casting up stones, obeying
    the commands of a skilled huntsman
who mutters when roused at dawn.
    They headed for a group of tents
where they thought they'd trap
    the quarry. "Onward!" their handler
shouted, and the throng of killers
    advanced, keeping their heads low.
Suddenly they were racing back,
    driving the oryx hard
in a dawn raid on a foreign clan—
    though their raid was as unique
as Ḥajr is unlike Ṣunaybiʿāt.
    At day's end they hadn't lost
their edge, full of bloodlust—
    still wild despite all their training.
At top speed, they pounced
    on the oryx—if you'd seen the bucks
lying in groups in the dust,
    you'd know they were doomed,
scuppered like large cargo
    ships decorated with cowries.
Our asses carried the slain
    animals strapped on their backs.
Once, these oryx roamed free—
    how close is death to life!

* *

24.48 In service to the best of men,
    our caliph, vanquisher of foes.

25

Abū l-Najm al-ʿIjlī: Coils Scraping on Coils

Under Umm al-ʿAmr's spell, 25.1
I was kept from visiting her
by the palace guards—
her lord being a jealous
brute. Shapely
and full below the waist,
she wears ear-
rings that grace
her slender neck;
her lovely face,
the wondrous work
of the Creator, shines
as bright as the sun's
morning rays;
as she sleeps, the air
is filled with Dārīn
musk and ambergris,
as fragrant as a young
bride's perfume.

* *

The camels in calf 25.12
refusing the drover

their milk, he relied
  on those that lactated
all year round.
  He had watched the stars
for signs of rain
  and brought his herd
to the flat grasslands
  where the plants were fed
by the first showers.

* *

25.17 As her horns dug up
  the *arṭā* tree's
roots, the dry
  and the moist, in a copse
heavy with fruit
  like unripe dates,
she shone a brilliant
  white. Into the thicket
she retreated, away
  from the scorching wind.

* *

25.23 Over the hills and hard
  ground a lean
jack drove
  his harem, compliant,
then resistant,
  until they began to molt,
revealing back muscles
  and sorrel stripes,
silk-white barrels,
  hip creases bright
as cotton; whinnying,
  their teeth looked

like the molars of a camel 25.30
past her due date,
grinding her teeth
at night. The shrubs
lost their sap
and the jennies' croups
changed color;
worn out from mating,
tails no longer matted
and moist with sweat,
they rejected the jacks.
The jack brayed,
sounding the call
to water—an overspill
from a mountain pool
fed by a plentiful
spring: they waded
in its clear waters,
like young women
walking briskly
down the road. All night,
the hunter paid
no heed to the viper
nesting in the corner
of his dugout;
it shrank from him,
coils scraping 25.43
on coils like a millstone
grinding barley,
hissing as loud
as a whelp's whine,
threatening to strike,
like twigs crackling
in a flaming oven.

25.50 Accustomed to snakes
hissing at him in their nest
like sheepdogs barking
to protect their herd,
he knew he was safe
from its rage; he valued
his life and was certain
of his soul's fate
in this world and the next—
after death his soul
would be resurrected
and he'd live again.
In his left hand
he gripped a bow
of *nab'* wood, its
tight string
aimed at the kill spot;
the bow was full
at the grip, curved,
arced back, its low
thrum making it
hard to hear;
25.59 his right hand
fetched an arrow
from his quiver, its head
whetted till it gleamed,
its fletches smeared
with blood; he knew
he could control the arrow
speeding straight
to the throat. He'd dug
a deep hideout
and roofed it over as best
he could, with space

to raise the bow
    and pull it taut.
He fired: the jenny's 25.66
    nostrils snorted
twice. His pots
    of meat were welcomed—
he had no wish to preserve
    the jenny's flesh,
thinking only of the joys
    that praise bestows
upon the soul.

May the Tamīm in Sadīr's 25.70
    rocks and wells
perish in their droves!

26

Abū l-Najm al-ʿIjlī: The Hills Shimmered

26.1 Flirtatious women,
all frivolous talk and bright
kohled eyes, were the death
of me, the *arāk* tooth
sticks in their mouths softened
by saliva as cool as Euphrates
water mixed with smooth
jiryāl-red wine.

* *

26.7 I exhausted my mighty camels
by crossing the unpeopled desert,
uncharted and bare; the jinn
in its loops and twists wept
at how arid it was—a land forcing
the spindly ostrich into its shelter.

* *

26.12 It was harvest time: the farmers
had trimmed the palms and lowered
their baskets; the hills shimmered
in the haze like chunks of meat
floating in a pot of fat.

The onagers longed for the water
hole while, with their cousin the jack,
they climbed hill after hill
through valleys and uplands,
wrapped in a dust cloud
in Bayḍah, separating the soil
from the fodder, the jack's
cheeks dyed bright
safflower red from the plants
he'd eaten. He chose a strong, 26.22
compliant, stout-bodied jenny,
striking her with his shank to make
her run, covering the valley's
slopes in a cloak of stones:
she left her family behind—
the one-year-olds, the freshly
weaned, the herd's newborn,
and the aggressive, hard-running jack,
his violent bray as loud
as the roar of a thick-necked
bull camel who's serviced his harem.
His bites had scarred her rump,
previously untouched, as they grazed
in Quryān's hills on tall
flowering bromegrass drenched
by the rain, unspoiled by the dirt
washed up by the showers. The herd
reached water at midday,
huddled over their shadows,
the mountain peaks burning
under a sun that blazed as if a fire
were dragging both ends of its rope;

they gulped the water from the cold
pool in a wadi's hollow
as quickly as a lanky ostrich
sprinting to her chicks. They drank
till the tardy sun set,
as weak as a putrid eye.
26.43 In a blind with wattled gaps
hid Asmā''s husband:
her thin arms were blackened
by lifting pots and roasting
meat in hot coals—her man
was such a skilled hunter
she thought she owned the asses
of Liwā. He spent a night
of terror nested among snakes,
the horned viper talking to him
by scraping its muscular coils
like a millstone revolving
above the mat, like a mangy
camel rubbing against a hobble.
He yearned like a lover for the viper
to stop, but saw no point
in quitting his hideout. His hand
clasped a curved bow
that thrummed in his grip, pining
for its darts like a mother camel
groaning for her weaned calf.
He aimed at the onager's flank,
next to the spleen: the shafts
were ready—he'd fitted their heads.
In the dark he felt in his quiver
for the heavy arrows he'd whetted
to a pale-gray sheen, their feathers

bloody from clots coughed up
    by slain onagers. At the end
of target practice, his arrows
    lay scattered on the ground
having shot through their bodies.
    Like a swarm of locusts, the herd
bolted—there were too many kills to count.

27

ʿAbd al-Ḥamīd al-Kātib: To the Beat of the Drums

An epistle on the hunt, unrivaled in its subject matter.

27.1 May God by the gift of His grace and the comfort of His blessings and the succor of His majesty perpetuate the reign of our Supreme Commander.

On our expedition we enjoyed more favor, good fortune, success, and pleasure than God has ever granted to any hunter or devotee of the chase. So much game, such a fine hunt, so many beasts taken—to say nothing of how agreeable our trek was, how easy our goal was to achieve, and how many of us proved our mettle on that day. Of course, the game scampered and ran hard for safety, so we experienced all the fatigues of the chase as we ran them down to enjoy the benefits they bring us. They were so fleet, their scurries so intense, the paths they took so scattered that we were worn out by the pursuit and frustrated by the river, but in the end we savored the unalloyed delight of victory.

27.2 Sire, on the expedition we took the readiest hunting birds and best-trained dogs, all of the noblest species, largest physiques, sharpest claws, mightiest limbs, and most attractive colorings. Habituated to the hardships of the chase, familiar with local waymarks and stopping places, and acquainted with all the coverts of the quarry, these animals had been raised wonderfully well—their behavior in the field reflected their training. We were mounted on precious *shihrī* horses, renowned for their spirit and pedigree, their speed and hardiness.

We stalked our quarry skillfully, at a gentle trot. It had been raining and the ground was covered with plants and grasses, so wet that the winds did not sting and our horses' hooves did not kick up any dust. Eventually, by the time we had traveled several bowshots' distance, the sun rose in the sky and dawn suffused the clouds. The trees shone like pearls and the flowers sparkled and laughed. It was a spectacularly beautiful sight—the sun smiling, revealing lush fields in full bloom. Our sprightly horses strained at the reins and stretched out into a canter. Then a mist enfolded us, clinging to us before drifting away, blocking our field of vision and obscuring the safe approaches. We were moving through an area of soft, sandy soil with thick, tangled trees, where the mountain passes were covered in greenery. It was full of game—gazelles, foxes, and hares. Our destination was a wooded region where wild animals and game were known to gather. So carefully had we been following the tracks, so focused were we on stalking the quarry that we had moved beyond the trees and were spread out across a section of hard, stony ground.

We looped back to where we had started. The mist had lifted and we were now able to see clearly. We spotted a herd of rhim gazelles grazing at their leisure: the mist had concealed us and our advance had been muffled by the lushness of the fields. Despite how difficult it was to see anything at such a great distance, the dogs spotted them straightaway and tugged at their leashes. The birds shook their wings. Confident of their flight and speed in pursuit, I gave the order for them to be cast. Like the whisper of the wind, the birds skimmed the surface of the earth, scowling as they tracked them, choosing the best animals and sinking their talons deep. The quarry scattered like locusts in a gale. Some hid in their coverts. Shouts and halloos, commands and calls filled the air as the handlers urged on their dogs by name. The gazelles, running to the right and left in terror, bleated as they sped away from their pursuers, some dying on the end of a spear, some kicking up their hooves in an attempt to defend themselves. Drunk on power, surfeited with game, we were astounded by such abundance. How generous are the blessings of God!

27.3 Led by an experienced and skillful guide who knew the way through the watercourses, we proceeded to a large pond in a green meadow, surrounded by a tangle of trees of all hues and shades, packed with all kinds of birds, all strangers to man—no one had hunted there before. The drums were beaten and the trumpets sounded the death call. The sky was full of birds. The raptors were excited by the flapping of their wings. The goshawks sped off on the chase, the sakers dived into the attack, and the peregrines were brutal, racing hard through the air and impaling them on their talons. In the end, covered in gore like a squadron that has fulfilled its mission or a raiding party that has vanquished its foes, we grew weary of the slaughter. Our birds had triumphed over quarry great and small, the weak mixed in with the strong. We could scarcely contain our joy and were ecstatic for the rest of the day. How generous are the blessings of God!

27.4 Then, my lord, we headed to a region where the game was described as plentiful and the fields a delight to the eye. But we had been misinformed and the description was inaccurate—when we arrived, we could see neither game nor vegetation and there was nothing to delight our eyes. We next crossed an area of stony ground and flat desert. Despairing of flushing any game, our enthusiasm flagged, but then we spotted a bulky jack standing over a pool of water by a dense bunch of low-hanging branches in front of a large drove of onagers. We made for him and launched our attack on his harem on foot and on horseback. He brayed and whinnied repeatedly. His jennies, twisting and taking fright at the dreadful sight, turned and bolted as if let loose. The chase was hard and tiring—as we followed their tracks we had to stay alert to the danger of all the holes in the ground, all the soft sand, and all the obstacles in our way. The chase took us to the edge of a fearsome wadi where a river flowed, its banks thick with trees. The onagers, first to arrive, had taken cover among the foliage. We arranged the horses like beads on a string and, to the beat of the drums and a chorus of shouts, a number of horsemen charged and scattered them, sorting them according to their condition. The end was inevitable. Praised be God at all times!

Note to the English Translation

Poem 1: Imru' al-Qays: Echoes of Love Lost

Imru' al-Qays ("the devotee of the god Qays") ibn Ḥujr was a prince of the house of Kindah, a tribe that ruled eastern Arabia in the first half of the sixth century AD. He was known as "the wandering prince" (*al-malik al-ḍillīl*) and "the man of sores" (*dhū l-qurūḥ*). Ḥujr, king of Kindah, was killed in an uprising led by a subject tribe, the Banū Asad. Legends proliferated concerning Imru' al-Qays's attempts to muster an army from surrounding courts, including Constantinople, to regain his father's throne. Many sources aver that the poet was dead by AD 550. According to one version, he died in the vicinity of Ankara, when he put on a poisoned shirt given to him by the emperor Justinian.

This qasida, one of the *Muʿallaqāt*, "the Suspended Odes," is arguably the most famous poem in Arabic. It is also one of the oldest pre-Islamic poems to have been preserved, dating from about the middle of the sixth century. Few other poets in the tradition have matched Imru' al-Qays's tragic and grandiloquent character, preserved so clearly in the lore surrounding the poem.

The bravura of the poetic performance, with its three principal themes of love, the hunt, and the storm, has seldom been equaled. The poem crackles with a fierce energy. It is episodic and relies on parataxis: one sequence or vignette follows another, each bursting with power, replete with dazzling images, and delivered in the unmistakable voice of its composer. Yet this paratactical style presents us with an enigma—what, if anything, is the basic subject of the poem? Many readers have been content simply to relish each line and luxuriate in their poetic grandeur. Others, under the spell of the poet's charm, have read the piece as an expression of his male potency, his amorous and hunting exploits culminating in a storm scene, a topic that seems to have functioned in the Jahiliya as a showcase for poetic prowess. (See Poem 3 for another example of a storm scene, and my notes.) Still others have construed the poem in terms of the lore surrounding the poet and have argued that it is a song of vengeance, a declaration of the poet's resolve to avenge the death of his father and claim his filial right to the throne of Kindah. Of course, none of these readings excludes the others, and each is in its way a sensitive response to the qasida's content.

I read the poem both as an echo chamber of frustrated memories and as a song of rage, a rage so fierce it threatens to tear apart the fabric of society and wreak destruction upon the land. After a scene in which the poet, on a desert journey or raid, is stopped in his tracks by the tears brought to his eyes by his memories of a long-lost happiness, there comes a long section of *fakhr* (boast) in which the poet sings of his amorous conquests. The decay brought to these former tribal encampments and their reclamation by nature has produced a wasteland that is matched by the outrageous violation of tribal taboos in his dealings with women: his grandiose and reckless sacrifice of his camel; his seduction of ʿUnayzah in her camel-borne litter; and his indulgent abandonment to the sensual beauty of Fāṭimah, so condemned by his comrades. Other poets may boast of their feats on the battlefield; Imru' al-Qays wages his war on the women of the tribe.

The axis of the qasida is the description of the night of anxiety passed by the sleepless poet as he watches the stars crawl across the sky and his encounter with the wolf—the poet is no longer a member of his tribe, but is itinerant, indigent, and luckless. In his celebration of erotic conquest, the poet has torn his tribe apart and is now completely on his own.

His next task is to bring destruction to the natural world, which he achieves by training and harnessing the power of nature in the form of his fearsome horse and by annihilating a herd of oryx. In the pre-Islamic imaginary, the horse is regularly associated with water; indeed, it was thought to derive its power from water, often from rain. By taming and channeling the raging torrent of his horse, the poet makes himself a master of the element of water.

The royal hunt was intended to ensure prosperity and fertility for a ruler's people, and this hunt certainly provides his comrades with a feast of meat. But this is a royal hunt conducted by an outcast, perhaps even a king deprived of his rightful throne, and it unleashes a destructive surfeit of fertility in the form of a cataclysmic storm that, if we follow the toponyms in the poem, floods almost all of Najd. In this qasida, the fertility brought by the rain to the desert lands (the fertility we also find in, for example, the *Muʿallaqah* of ʿAntarah ibn Shaddād) is forestalled—the poet instead offers us the startling image of drowned beasts of prey floating like uprooted bulbs of the sea onion (*Drimia maritima*). This is a flood of apocalyptic dimensions. We are left wondering whether the rage is a rage for vengeance—a demand for a throne lost through regicide—or whether it echoes the poet's memories of frustrated ambition.

The poem also represents the earliest extant example of a complete hunting scene in the manner that would later emerge as central to the *ṭardiyyah* genre: it begins with the early-morning departure of the hunter and the hunting expedition, it describes in fine detail the nonhuman (the horse) that the poet-hunter must co-opt in order to achieve a successful hunt, it contains an account of the chase and the kill, and it culminates in a communal feast.

The following studies of the poem may be of interest: Farrin, "The Triumph of Imru' al-Qays," in *Abundance from the Desert: Classical Arabic Poetry*, 1–24; Jamil, *Ethics and Poetry in Sixth-Century*

Arabia; Stetkevych, "Regicide and Retribution: The *Muʿallaqah* of Imru' al-Qays," in *The Mute Immortals Speak: Pre-Islamic Poetry and the Poetics of Ritual*, 241–86; and Stetkevych and Stetkevych, "The *Muʿallaqah* of Imru' al-Qays: Adventures of Youthful Passion."

*

Imru' al-Qays's warhorse, a vortex of motion, shares a cosmic intensity with Ted Hughes's monumental nonhumans in "The Horses" (1957): "Huge in the dense grey—ten together— / Megalith-still." I learned from Robyn Creswell that Alfred, Lord Tennyson modeled his dramatic monologue "Locksley Hall" (1835), a meditation on lost love, the progress of civilization, and the noble savage, on the *Muʿallaqah* of Imru' al-Qays.

Poem 2: ʿAbīd ibn al-Abraṣ: That Mighty Hunter the Eagle

ʿAbīd ibn al-Abraṣ (the Son of the Leper, or Albino), known as Abū Dūdān or Abū Ziyād, an important member of the Banū Saʿd ibn Thaʿlabah, part of the Asad tribe, lived in the first half of the sixth century AD. ʿAbīd seems to have played a major role when his clan rebelled against Kindite ascendancy during the reign of their king Ḥujr ibn al-Ḥārith, a rebellion that resulted in the king's death. This act made him an enemy of Ḥujr's son, Imru' al-Qays. ʿAbīd was reckoned among the "methuselahs" of the Jahiliya, and one account has him put to death by al-Mundhir III ibn Mā' al-Samā' (d. AD 554), Lakhmid ruler of Ḥīrah.

This qasida, another of the *Muʿallaqāt*, "the Suspended Odes," is a profound and majestic meditation on loss, aging, and the triumph of Fate over humankind. The destruction of the poet's people and the desolation of their tribal encampments lead into a sequence of adages. The poet then describes the terrors of the desert journeys he has undertaken in search of his vanished tribe, and his concise camel description culminates in a celebration of exploits on the field of battle. The poem is famous for its comparison of the poet's warhorse with an eagle, the earliest extant example in Arabic of such a comparison, and a theme (horse = raptor) that would resurface in the work of poets working within the developed *ṭardiyyah* tradition. The eagle's brutal hunt of the fox is emblematic of the inexorability of Fate the hunter, whose depredations are explored with such pathos in the early sections of the poem.

Composed in a meter that has only one parallel in the early corpus, a meter identified as a shortened form of *basīṭ*, the qasida's metrical idiosyncrasy has occasioned some perplexity in transmitters and critics (see Larsen, "The *Muʿallaqah* of ʿAbīd ibn al-Abraṣ: Meditations on Life," 456). The version of the text preserved by al-Tibrīzī retains an unmetrical sequence in verse 9 and verse 13, which I have decided not to emend based on the other extant versions of the text (see Lyall's discussion, *The Dīwāns*, 5 (Arabic), and Nöldeke's note quoted by Lyall, *The Dīwāns*, 11–12 (Arabic)). The other versions of the poem also contain varying sequences of verses, alternatives to that preserved by al-Tibrīzī. The Islamic tone of verses 18b–21 occasioned considerable debate (Lyall's views, *The Dīwāns*, 8 (English), are representative).

On ʿAbīd's poem, see Montgomery, "Dichotomy in *Jāhilī* Poetry," and Larsen, "The *Muʿallaqah* of ʿAbīd ibn al-Abraṣ."

*

ʿAbīd's eagle immediately brings to mind Walt Whitman's "The Dalliance of the Eagles" in *Leaves of Grass*, a closely observed impression of what is probably a territorial battle, interpreted by the poet as "rushing amorous contact."

Poem 3: ʿAbīd ibn al-Abraṣ: The Seas of Poetry

This poem is singular in the Jahiliya corpus for its sequence of themes (storm scene, followed by extended simile, followed by boast), its magnificent central description of the poet's poetic prowess in a comparison with the leviathan, and its lexicon and alliterative wordplay (for example, the repetition of the root *m-l-ṣ* in line 15). Lyall, *The Dīwāns*, 51, declares the poem to be "of doubtful authenticity." My hunch is that the poem comes from an eastern Arabian tradition, vestiges of which can still be discerned many centuries later in extant Nabati poetry.

The poet begins with a sonorous evocation of a lightning storm and desert flood, in many respects reminiscent of the vernacular poetry of the early modern Emirati poet al-Māyidī ibn Ẓāhir (*Love, Death, Fame: Poetry and Lore from the Emirati Oral Tradition*, Poems 2 ("Lightning's Laughter"), 8 ("Rain Poem"), and especially 16 ("Intelligent Speech and Borders of the Land")). ʿAbīd next sings of his poetic skills, and the poem concludes with a celebration of his honor couched in terms of abstinence from food when on a raid, accompanied by a biting attack on a sponger whose eagerness to rely on the provisions, bravery, and generosity of others is condemned. This lampoon is very much in the style of the withering attacks on his contemporaries composed by the eighteenth-century Najd poet Ḥmēdān al-Shwēʿir (see *Arabian Satire: Poetry from 18th-Century Najd*).

*

In certain respects, this qasida reminds me of Amy Lowell's "The Pike" (1914) and John Montague's "The Trout" (1967), with hints of the Anglo-Saxon poem "The Whale," but on another level I hear affinities with Imtiaz Dharker's "Arc" (2018): "Words / are the pearl. Dive for them / and we become real."

Poem 4: Al-Muraqqish al-Akbar: When Vultures Enter the Tents

ʿAmr (or ʿAwf or Rabīʿah) ibn Mālik (d. AD 550?) was a member of Ḍubayʿah ibn Qays ibn Thaʿlabah, part of the powerful Bakr ibn Wāʾil super-tribe. His byname al-Muraqqish (the Embellisher) was perhaps given to him because of his use of the verb *raqqasha* in line 2 of this poem, though it has been suggested that the name is actually Muraqqish (without the definite article), possibly an

Arabicized version of the Greek name Markos. Al-Muraqqish's family was renowned for their poets: his father was a famous poet; his nephews were the poets ʿAmr ibn Qamīʾah (d. ca. AD 570), Bishr ibn ʿAmr (fl. late sixth century), and al-Muraqqish al-Aṣghar (that is, al-Muraqqish the Younger) (d. ca. AD 570); he was great-uncle to Ṭarafah ibn al-ʿAbd (d. between AD 554 and 569), composer of one of the *Muʿallaqāt*; and cousin to al-Aʿshā Maymūn ibn Qays (d. 8/629 or 9/630), composer of another of the *Muʿallaqāt*. Al-Muraqqish was famous in later centuries for his love for Asmāʾ, which became the stuff of legend. He is said to have been taught how to write by the Christians of Ḥīrah.

This qasida connects him with the power struggle in the first half of the sixth century AD between the Kindite kings of Ḥajr (modern-day Riyadh) and the Lakhmid rulers of Ḥīrah. It is an unusual poem, written in a rare version of the meter *sarīʿ*, replete with many words whose meanings were obscure to the commentators, and with an elliptical, almost at times clipped syntax that can make it difficult to understand. Its principal subject matter is also obscure, as it presents a case addressed to a powerful overlord in defense of the poet's tribe, who are apparently accused of involvement in a raid. The sequence of the poem's themes is also unusual, so much so that some scholars have argued that the qasida is a composite of two separate poems, conjoined by virtue of sharing the same meter and rhyme scheme.

The poem is informed by a military context: the desert ruin scene is followed by the departure of the litter-borne women of the tribe (a motif with military overtones in the corpus), and this is juxtaposed with a lament for the poet's kinsman unburied on the field of battle—presumably a casualty in the raid described in the second half of the poem. The lament includes a rare instance of the death of one of the qasida's iconic nonhumans, in this case an ibex, in a pattern that would be used in laments by the poets of Hudhayl (see further examples in Poems 6 and 9). The poet next pleads the innocence of his tribe by attributing the raid to a king of Kindah (or Jafnah, depending on how we explain the relevance of the Ghassānids in the poem) and by reminding the addressee of the kinship between the poet's tribe and him, intoning the glory of his clan, and, by implication, demanding the blood vengeance for Thaʿlabah.

According to Lyall, the "poem gives a strong impression of antiquity," and this may well be the case. Perhaps it belongs to a Najdi qasida tradition that did not become normative and is therefore a relic of a lost style. Whatever the truth of the poem's antiquity, I have included it here because of its depiction of the death of the ibex.

A few details of the poem require some clarification. The "saffron princesses" are the princesses of the house of Kindah, who would apparently daub their bodies with saffron; "uncircumcised men" is a reference to Ghalfā, the son of al-Ḥārith, king of Kindah. There is some confusion over the reading "Jafnah," by which the Ghassānid phylarchs of Syria are usually meant: their relevance to al-Muraqqish's tribal politics is not obvious. I agree with Lyall that we should read "Kindah." The penultimate foot of this line has an extra syllable in addition to the variations permitted in the later scansion of the meter, but as this syllabic pattern (short/short/long/short/long) recurs in verse 21, it is presumably a pattern acceptable in the version of *sarīʿ* al-Muraqqish was employing. On these somewhat obscure verses, see Lyall, *The Mufaḍḍaliyyāt*, 2:184nn18–19.

For a study of the poem, see Nathaniel Miller, "Tribal Poetics in Early Arabic Culture: The Case of Ashʿār al-Hudhaliyyīn," 139–41, 340–44.

*

Al-Muraqqish's doomed ibex exudes an air of tragic mystery similar to that which envelops the nonhumans in Robert Penn Warren's poem "The Caribou" (1984).

Poem 5: Al-Shanfarā: Like a Spleen-Dark Wolf

Almost nothing is known for certain about the poet al-Shanfarā ("The Man with Large Lips"). His name was apparently Thābit (or ʿAmr) ibn Mālik. His tribal affiliation is unclear, but it plays an important role in the lore surrounding his life as the tradition seeks to explain why the poet was outlawed from his natal clan. The sources accordingly record a variety of genealogies. The dominant version connects him with a clan of Azd, while one genealogy states that he was born into the Banū Salāmān ibn Mufrij, a clan of Mālik ibn Zahrān. This source goes on to affirm that al-Shanfarā's father was killed by a fellow tribesman and that his father's tribe refused to sanction the application of the law of vengeance in this case. As a consequence, al-Shanfarā waged war on his tribe and allied himself with his maternal clan, the Banū Shabābah of Qays ʿAylān. Another, cognate, tradition alleges that al-Shanfarā avenged the death of his father by killing his father's murderer, Ḥarām ibn Jābir al-Salāmānī, during the pre-Islamic pilgrimage season at Minā, even though Ḥarām's blood was deemed inviolable, as the assassination occurred during one of the four "sacrosanct" (*ḥurum*) months of the pagan year, during which warfare was forbidden. These versions of the Shanfarā legend seek to account for why the poet is numbered as one of the fabled *ṣaʿālīk*, the so-called brigand or outlaw (that is, tribeless) poets, of the Jahiliya. Al-Shanfarā is said to have been killed in an ambush in the mountains south of Mecca.

This poem, known in Arabic as *lāmiyyat al-ʿarab* (the desert Arab poem rhyming in *lām*—the letter *l*), is among the most feted qasidas in the pre-Islamic corpus. It is unique in the corpus, its vocabulary so obscure and its tenor so idiosyncratic that for centuries it has been the subject of controversy, many scholars questioning its authenticity and arguing that it is a second-/eighth-century forgery. While the poem, like its poet, is shrouded in mystery, there is no denying the magnificent sweep of its virtuosic performance, the searing intensity of its similes and imagery, the implacable wrath and savagery of its cadences, and the gloriously paratactic density of its thought.

The poet begins with an address of his nearest kin, his "brothers," literally the "sons of my mother." He urges them to join him on a night raid. It is through raiding and martial prowess that men win greatness on earth and achieve the honor that secures them inviolability from the depredations of foes. Should his kin decide not to join his raid, the poet declares that he has other comrades in arms to turn to, in the shape of three nonhumans: the wolf, the desert viper, and the hyena. Unlike his natal group, these comrades will not betray or punish him for his misdeeds. The poet now turns to sing of his hardiness on raiding missions, displaying his nobility through a reluctance to partake of the group's provisions, and he celebrates the efficacy of his weapons: a sword and a bow, equipment matched only by his "bold heart." He next launches into a sequence of self-praise, in which he compares himself favorably with a series of good-for-nothings, members of a tribe who contribute nothing to its well-being, thereby declaring his importance to his brothers: once again, raiding provides the context for this sequence. This boast is concluded by the poet's justification for why he will keep aloof from his kin—if they bring him shame, his "bitter soul" will refuse to compromise.

A wonderful wolf simile and a dazzling scene in which the poet races against a flock of sandgrouse to arrive at a pool of water continue the self-praise and lead the poet to describe his current situation: "exiled for crimes," haunted by cares, and hunted by those out to exact revenge upon him. His quest to escape his plight, and presumably to exact vengeance in his turn, leads him to roam the deserts, foraging for sustenance in a state of extreme poverty.

The poet's crimes, the acts for which he has been exiled, are conveyed in a brutal sequence in which he goes "to widow wives and orphan / children," in a nocturnal assassination that leaves the people of al-Ghumayṣāʾ bewildered. As a consequence of these murders, the poet must seek safety by taking refuge on a mountain in a remote desert—but as the squalor of his appearance and the state of his hair indicates, he remains beyond the pale of society—his own quest for vengeance is unfinished.

The poet concludes his qasida with a startling picture in which a herd of ibex nannies circumambulate him, just as maidens in trailing, fringed gowns circumambulate a stone idol. Al-Shanfarā, the pariah, has become divine, scaling the mountain heights like an ibex billy, in an image that is reminiscent of the ibex that appear so frequently on Ḥimyarite monuments and epigraphy.

I have included this poem for several reasons: it hinges on the notion that man is hunted by Fate, and in al-Shanfarā's case, hunted for his crimes; it highlights the centrality of blood vengeance to the hunting complex; and its vivid nonhuman episodes prefigure the attention to detail and the micro-scale relationality of many of the descriptions of nonhuman hunters found in the developed *ṭardiyyah* genre. This qasida has always been one of my favorite pre-Islamic poems.

A few details of the poem require some elucidation: "the sticks of a honey gatherer / high on the rock face" means that the wild bees build their hive on a rock face and the honey gatherer climbs above the hive, or is let down to it by ropes, and uses a long stick to safely extract the honeycomb. The "bone dice tossed / by gamers" describes dice made from the knuckles or talus bones of sheep (astragali); the wider context is probably a reference to astragalomancy, a type of cleromancy. The commentators suggest that by "daughter of the dunes" the poet intends either a snake or an oryx doe.

On the poem, see Stetkevych, "Archetype and Attribution: Al-Shanfarā and the *Lāmiyyat al-ʿArab*," in *The Mute Immortals Speak*, 119–60; Farrin, "An Outcast Replies," in *Abundance from the Desert*, 25–45; and El-Ariss, "Return of the Beast: From Pre-Islamic Ode to Contemporary Novel." See Fahd, "Nasr," for the ibex as representation of the South Arabian divinity Ilumḳuh.

*

Al-Shanfarā's wolves have much in common with Ted Hughes's "The Howling of Wolves" (1967), while his sandgrouse make me think of John Clare's "The Reed Bird" (1835–37) or Paul Muldoon's "Plovers" (1998).

Poem 6: Ṣakhr al-Ghayy: The Workings of Fate

Ṣakhr ibn ʿAbdallāh, known as al-Ghayy (the Unruly), was a member of a branch of Hudhayl, the tribal confederation that occupied the region around Mecca. He was the brother of a bandit or outlaw poet, al-Aʿlam al-Hudhalī, and presumably took part in his brigandish exploits. Almost nothing is known of him beyond his poetic activities, in particular a series of flytings he exchanged with a fellow tribesman, Abū l-Muthallam. He is thought to have been alive ca. AD 600.

This sonorous and dignified elegy for a brother killed by a snake contains two striking episodes. In the first, an ibex is killed by an indigent hunter desperate to feed his father and keep him alive; in the second, an eagle, hunting to feed her chicks, breaks her wing as she launches an attack on a gazelle. There is thus a deft interweaving of the activities, aspirations, and frustrations of both humans and nonhumans. Both panels share obvious parallels with Poem 4 by al-Muraqqish al-Akbar and anticipate Abū Dhuʾayb's more celebrated elegy for his sons (Poem 9).

The poem is a meditation on the inexorability of Fate who, by virtue of being in control of our destinies, remorselessly hunts down humans and nonhumans alike. In this way, the poem sheds light on how, in the hunting complex, humankind is stalked by Fate. We are reminded that in these passages it is not simply a question of subsistence hunting or of the royal hunt as ritual and ceremony, but with the existential anxiety that so typifies the early Arabic qasida and persists, however modified by faith, into the Islamic era.

I have included the poem partly on account of its affinities with the other poems, and partly because Ṣakhr al-Ghayy's nonhumans rival those of al-Shanfarā in Poem 5, but principally because the poet imbues the ibex and eagle with genuine grandeur and pathos, a mood I have tried to capture by using a loosely articulated, six-beat line.

For a study of the poem, see Nathaniel Miller, "Tribal Poetics," 348–53.

*

The vulnerability and resonance of Ṣakhr al-Ghayy's tragic nonhumans contrast with the otherness of Denise Levertov's nonhumans in "Come into Animal Presence" (1960), or even Elizabeth Bishop's "The Moose" (1972), in which everything, including the chatter of the elderly couple as they gossip about life and death on a bus ride in Nova Scotia, is brought to a stark halt as a moose crosses the road in front of the bus.

Poem 7: Labīd ibn Rabīʿah: In the Grip of the North Wind

Abū ʿAqīl Labīd ibn Rabīʿah was one of the "methuselahs" of the pre-Islamic and early Islamic era. A member of the Banū Jaʿfar ibn Kilāb, a clan of the ʿĀmir ibn Ṣaʿṣaʿah, he participated in a tribal delegation to the court of the Lakhmid ruler al-Nuʿmān ibn Māʾ al-Samāʾ II (r. ca. AD 580–602) in Ḥīrah, an indication that he was already a well-established poet by the beginning of the seventh century. Labīd also participated in his tribe's delegation to Prophet Muḥammad in Medina in 9/630. During this visit, he is said to have become a Muslim. According to one report, he is said to have composed no more poetry after his conversion, though this is manifestly not the case: many of the threnodies he composed for his dead brother, Arbad, reveal a close familiarity with Qurʾanic eschatology. Labīd is said to have died in Kufa ca. 40/660–61.

This qasida, one of the *Muʿallaqāt*, is a powerful celebration of the pre-Islamic Arabian ethos. The themes of each movement of the qasida—the deserted tribal dwellings (*aṭlāl*), the camel description with its onager and oryx tableaux (*waṣf al-nāqah*), and the tribal boast (*fakhr*)—are meticulously explored, as the poet progresses from desolation to tribal community, charting both his personal merits and the glory of his kinsfolk.

The centerpiece of the qasida is the nonhuman narratives of the onagers and the oryx doe. Both creatures face hardship and prove triumphant. The onagers are successful in their race to the water hole. The oryx doe loses her fawn and, while searching for her offspring killed by wolves, defeats a hunter and his dogs, running at least two dogs through with her horns. Labīd's qasida reminds us that our existence is dominated by the perilous hunt—no creature is ever simply a hunter: all are hunter and hunted, for, as the poet sings, one day "Death will trap my soul." Human worth and value consist not in immortality but in the perpetuation of the glory that a clan inherits from its ancestors and to which it adds by means of acts of generosity, deeds of valor, and unwavering dedication to the demands of blood vengeance.

In this qasida, Labīd gives to posterity a monumental poetic celebration of his clan's power and dignity, the like of which few tribes could match. Little wonder then that, upon hearing Labīd recite his qasida, a fellow poet is reported to have declared him "the greatest poet of the desert Arabs."

For an informed appreciation of the poem, with translation, see Stetkevych and Stetkevych, "The *Muʿallaqah* of Labīd ibn Rabīʿah: The Mute Immortals."

*

Labīd's nonhumans are grandiose and spectacular, symbols of the supremacy of the poet and his tribe. His qasida makes me think of a number of poems in English, in terms of contrasting aesthetics: "Grongar Hill" (1726), John Dyer's prospect poem, for the dissonance of the topographies of both poems; D. H. Lawrence's "A Doe at Evening" (1917), in which the irruption of the doe into the poet's consciousness leads him to reflect on his masculinity, unlike Labīd, for whom the oryx and onager are vehicles for the magniloquent projection of his virility; and then Labīd's warhorse contrasts so strongly with Vicki Hearnes's horses, especially the wavering of human and nonhuman consciousnesses in her "Riding a Nervous Horse" (2008).

Poem 8: Al-Muzarrid: My Flood of Words

Al-Muzarrid is the sobriquet of Yazīd ibn Ḍirār, also called Abū Ḍirār or Abū l-Ḥusayn, a member of clan Saʿd, a branch of Dhubyān, part of the Ghaṭafān federation. The meaning of the word *muzarrid* is unclear: *zarad* is a "coat of mail" and *zarada* means "to throttle or squeeze the throat"; both meanings suit the vigor and thrust of the poet's invective style.

Al-Muzarrid was a *mukhaḍram* poet—that is, he was born in the Jahiliya and lived during the early caliphate. He took part in a tribal deputation to Medina in 9/630, presumably to declare allegiance to Prophet Muḥammad and thus effectively indicate his adherence to Islam. During the deputation, al-Muzarrid composed a panegyric in praise of the Prophet. His fame as a poet rested predominantly on his fearsome skill as a satirist. He was summoned before Caliph ʿUthmān (r. 23–35/644–656) to answer complaints made by a tribe he had attacked: tribal invectives were easily capable of provoking unrest in the early polity. Al-Muzarrid renounced invective and received a caution from the caliph. Ibn al-Anbārī and his authorities attribute this poem to two of al-Muzarrid's brothers who were also poets: al-Shammākh ibn Ḍirār (d. after 30/650), and Jazʾ ibn Ḍirār (d. ?).

This qasida is simultaneously a bombastic boast and an admonitory invective. The poet begins with the themes of old age and his reluctant recovery from debilitating passion, with some exquisite verses describing Salmā, his beloved. Next follows a long boast in which the poet celebrates his martial prowess and sings the glories of his war gear: his warhorses, a steed and mare; his coat of mail, helmet, and neck armor; his swords and spear. The poet is thus the paragon of the northern Arabian mounted warrior knight. The poet then turns to his attackers, an unnamed group who have dared to besmirch his honor, despite his valor on the battlefield and his reputation for composing invectives that disgraced his foes forever. The final section of this mighty boast is the poet's portrait of an impoverished hunter who is unable to feed his family, a topic al-Muzarrid claims is so unsuitable for the qasida genre that it can only be rendered in verse by the most gifted of poets. The starving, doomed hunter provides a striking contrast to the resplendent warrior clad in all his military finery. This section is presumably also an implied threat: that by daring to attack the poet, his foes will face the same fate as the Ṣubāḥī hunter.

I have included this poem for its portrait of the starving hunter, a figure who also features in Poem 9 in this volume and who recurs regularly in the poems of Abū l-Najm al-ʿIjlī (Poems 22–26).

For studies of the poem, see Thomas Bauer, "Muzarrids Qaṣīde vom reichen Ritter und den armen Jäger," and Stetkevych, *The Hunt in Arabic Poetry: From Heroic to Lyric to Metapoetic*, 35–46.

*

It is to Anglo-Saxon poetry or old Welsh poetry that I turn for analogues to the audacity and sweep of al-Muzarrid's poem, in particular *The Book of Taliesin*, translated so powerfully by Gwyneth Lewis and Rowan Williams (2019). One can imagine the contours of the conversation between the starving hunter and his wife along the lines of Russel Edson's "Ape" (1973), in which father cries to mother, "I'm just saying that I'm damn sick of ape every night."

Poem 9: Abū Dhu'ayb: Fate the Hunter

Khuwaylid ibn Khālid Abū Dhu'ayb was a *mukhaḍram* poet, one who lived and composed poetry before the advent of Islam, and who survived and continued to compose after it. Like Ṣakhr al-Ghayy, he belonged to the Hijazi tribe of Hudhayl. He is thought to have become a Muslim when his tribe converted in 9/630, and he left the Hijaz for Egypt, where his five sons, whose death he laments in this poem, died in the plague of 17–18/638–40. Abū Dhu'ayb was part of the victorious expeditionary force that captured Ifrīqiyah in 26/647. He was charged with delivering the news to the caliph ʿUthmān (r. 23–35/644–56) in Medina but died on the journey.

This poem is a threnody for his fallen sons. Miller ("Tribal Poetics," 365–69) connects the poem with "a veritable genre of texts composed on the premise that young men's participation in the early Islamic conquests constituted filial disobedience" (369). The poet begins by laying before his audience the anguish of a father's grief, a passage unusual in early Arabic poetry for its exploration of the contours of the poet's emotion. The poet's defiant helplessness in the face of the depredations of Fate segue into three wonderful episodes: the onager jack and his harem slaughtered by a hunter lying in wait at the water hole, the oryx buck attacked and killed by a hunter and his hunting dogs, and the death in battle of two mighty champions who refuse to yield. Throughout the poem, Fate is seen to stalk and slay the creatures of the poet's world—the poet knows he is next, but will not be humbled. Abū Dhu'ayb's anger at his sons' disobedience by joining the conquests has been intensified by his grief over their death on the conquests. The final scene of futility in which the armored warriors kill each other assumes extra poignancy when we remember that Abū Dhu'ayb's sons died in the Islamic conquests of Egypt and North Africa.

The poem is clearly indebted to the lament of his fellow tribesman Ṣakhr al-Ghayy (Poem 6), a threnody in which both the ibex and the eagle die. What is less obvious, however, is that it is also indebted to Labīd's *Muʿallaqah* (Poem 7), in that it adumbrates that poem's opening scene of desolation and loss, follows it with onager and oryx episodes, and concludes with the theme of (the futility of) military valor and glory. The resultant composition is a hybrid, a *marthiyah* (threnody) patterned on the qasida structure typified by Labīd's great poem. Abū Dhu'ayb crystallizes the constituents of each of the three episodes and endows them with an air of timelessness, as can be seen from a comparison of the description of weapons in al-Muzarrid's poem (Poem 8) with Abū Dhu'ayb's description of ironclad champions. His setting and presentation are a distillation and consummation of the preceding poetic tradition.

The line sequences in the versions of this poem preserved in the *Mufaḍḍaliyyāt* and the Cairo manuscript of the poems of Hudhayl edited by Aḥmad al-Zayn differ from the version in al-Sukkarī's recension as edited here. Those versions also contain some additional lines.

A few of the details of the poem require some explanation. "Musharraq's shrine . . ." is an obscure line that has occasioned much discussion; Jones, *Early Arabic Poetry*, 2:211, suggests a link "to some pre-Islamic ritual" connected with litholatry. For the preferability of the reading *al-naẓm*, "Orion," instead of *al-najm*, "Pleiades," see Jones, *Early Arabic Poetry*, 2:218. The "gambler" in this instance is the individual who superintends the participants and so is pictured as hunched over the arrows once they've been cast to determine the results. The equine description of "grown fat / on milk" generated considerable debate, and Abū Dhu'ayb was attacked by some critics for contravening convention that maintained that a lean horse was the best for battle. In this instance, the mare has never been foaled; therefore, her udder is dry of milk and its teats hang like pendant earrings. She is so spirited that she refuses to yield her fastest speed when whipped, but will only do so of her own volition.

On the poem, see Stetkevych, "The ʿAyniyyah of Abū Dhu'ayb al-Hudhalī: The Achievement of a Classical Allegorical Form," and Hussein, "Two Sources for Abu Dhu'ayb al-Hudhali's Famous Elegy."

*

Abū Dhu'ayb's qasida makes me think of *The Gododdin*, in Gillian Clarke's luminous version (2021), and of Alice Oswald's *Memorial* (2011), her take on Homer's *Iliad*. The way death pervades the poem suggests Colin Simms's "Three Years in Glen Garry" (2015), with its relentless and staggering list of slaughter and death carried out between 1837 and 1840: "The Clearances were not only of the people, but of most of the other indigenes / at their climax."

Poem 10: Al-Ḥuṭay'ah: Slaughter Me, Father

Jarwal ibn Aws, known as al-Ḥuṭay'ah (the Homunculus), was a *mukhaḍram* poet, active before and after the advent of Islam, who is remembered in a colorful and striking body of lore in which are celebrated his stinginess, avarice, reluctance to follow Islamic rules about inheritance, and insouciance about the afterlife. There were apparently doubts over his paternity (he claimed descent from two different tribal groups) and he fell out with his brothers, both real and alleged, over his father's inheritance. He seems to have been of an acutely quarrelsome nature and was feared for his invectives of tribesmen and enemies alike. In fact, he fired off prickly invectives at his parents, siblings, tribes, wife, guests, and even himself. Al-Ḥuṭay'ah was one of the first poets to have supported himself entirely through patronage—his tack was to threaten a notable with an invective unless he was granted patronage, for which the notable would then be rewarded with a panegyric. The caliph 'Umar ibn al-Khaṭṭāb (r. 13–23/634–44) is said to have imprisoned him for one of his invectives and the poet was released on condition that he abstain from composing such poems, which he did for the rest of the caliph's reign. Al-Ḥuṭay'ah died between 41/661 and 54/674.

This poem by al-Ḥuṭay'ah (an attribution that has been questioned) is an adaptation of the indigent hunter theme familiar to us from al-Muzarrid's Poem 8. In it, a traveler in the deep desert chances upon a family that is so wild they seem to belong to the nonhuman rather than the human world. This family lives in extreme poverty, a poverty that the paterfamilias deems "a life of blessed ease." Of course, the arrival of a stranger demands an act of hospitality, but the family is so poor that they have nothing with which they can satisfy the rights of a guest. The eldest son offers his own body as the hospitable meal, in a moment reminiscent of Q Ṣāffāt 37:102, where Ismā'īl (Ishmael) tells Ibrāhīm (Abraham) he is willing to be his sacrifice. The head of the household comes close to accepting his son's offer but prays to God and sees his prayer answered by the successful kill of an onager jenny. The poem ends with a commensal feast and an extension of the family unit to include the traveler, who is, in fact, the poet who narrates this episode—he is clearly the itinerant guest who benefits from this instance of extreme Bedouin xenophilia. The poem also reminds us that, in terms of the hunting complex as developed in the Islamic centuries, the appearance of the quarry and the success of the hunt were considered to be signs of God's bounty, and God was responsible for replenishing the natural store of game.

For a study of the poem, see Stetkevych, *The Hunt*, 57–87 ("Sacrifice and Redemption: The Transformation of an Archaic Theme in al-Ḥuṭay'ah").

*

Hugh MacDiarmid's musings in "Parley of Beasts" (1933) on how "Auld Noah was at hame wi' them a'" (that is, with all the creatures on the Ark) suggest to me the profound idiosyncrasy of al-Ḥuṭay'ah's poem.

Poem 11: Ḥumayd al-Arqaṭ: A Tall-Necked Horse

Little is known about Ḥumayd al-Arqaṭ (the Leopard or the Speckled, an epithet often applied to the viper). He appears to have been connected to the retinue of the Umayyad governor of Iraq, al-Ḥajjāj ibn Yūsuf. One fragment is an attack on the counter-caliph ʿAbd Allāh ibn al-Zubayr and was presumably composed during al-Ḥajjāj's siege of Ibn al-Zubayr in Mecca in 72/691–92. A second fragment, composed sometime between 81/700 and 85/704–5, is connected with al-Ḥajjāj's campaign against the rebel Ibn al-Ashʿath. Like al-Ḥuṭay'ah, Ḥumayd composed an invective against a guest, a violation of the code of hospitality for which the tradition did not remember him fondly.

This poem, composed in *mashṭūr al-rajaz* (the dominant meter for the developed *ṭardiyyah* genre) was also attributed to Abū l-Najm al-ʿIjlī, the poet of Poems 22–26. It is preserved in the *Ḥamāsah*

(*Valor*), the magnificent collection of early Arabic poetry made by Abū Tammām (d. 231/845). The poem is a fascinatingly liminal composition, one that has the basic formal features of the developed *ṭardiyyah* genre but keeps resolutely within the pre-Islamic tradition—it is effectively a simile comparing a horse with a raptor in the manner of ʿAbīd in Poem 2. Indeed, were it not for the reference in the final line to the seeling of a raptor's eyes, a technique used to train a bird of prey such as a falcon or hawk by sewing its eyes shut, I'd think the bird described was an eagle, but I do not know for certain whether the practice of seeling was applied to eagles.

*

Ḥumayd's raptor has much in common with Ted Hughes's "Hawk Roosting" (1960): "There is no sophistry in my body: / My manners are tearing off heads."

Poems 12 and 13: Ghaylān ibn Ḥurayth: A Hunter since Her Youth and A Stipple-Cheeked Gos

Ghaylān ibn Ḥurayth is the most obscure of the poets included in this selection; so obscure, in fact, that we must resort to conjecture to suggest that he was active in the first decades of the second/eighth century. Even a scholar as knowledgeable in the poetic tradition as al-Shimshāṭī (fl. fourth/tenth c.) misattributes both poems to Abū Nuwās: in *Anwār*, 2:180, he includes Poem 12 in his section on the goshawk. This misattribution is corrected by Abū Nuwās's editor Ḥamzah al-Iṣbahānī (d. after 350/961), who quotes the first line and states that it should be ascribed to Ghaylān ibn Ḥurayth (Abū Nuwās, *Dīwān*, 2:325). Hämeen-Anttila, *Five Rağaz Collections*, 76, suggests that the similarities between Ghaylān's opening line and that of Abū Nuwās's cheetah poem (*Dīwān*, 2:285–87) may have led to the confusion. Hämeen-Anttila also notes that the opening line is similar to that of a dog poem by al-Nāshiʾ al-Akbar, included by al-Shimshāṭī in his anthology (*Anwār*, 2:129–30). Al-Shimshāṭī, *Anwār*, 2:181–82, also includes Poem 16 in his section on the goshawk, and again attributes it to Abū Nuwās, a misattribution that is once more corrected by Abū Nuwās's editor al-Iṣbahānī, who quotes the first line and states that it should be ascribed to Ghaylān ibn Ḥurayth (Abū Nuwās, *Dīwān*, 2:325). Hämeen-Anttila, *Five Rağaz Collections*, 77, notes that the opening line is similar to that of a goshawk poem by Abū Nuwās (*Dīwān*, 2:205–7). The ascription to Ghaylān is confirmed by Kushājim, who quotes verse 7 and an extra verse (7a) in his *Maṣāyid*, 68: "treading his left hand as if standing tall on a pulpit" (that is, after the phrase "an angry brute").

It is important to clear up the confusion because these two poems may in fact be the earliest extant examples of the *ṭardiyyah* in its developed form: on the basis of their evidence, the poetry of the obscure Ghaylān emerges as a pivotal moment in the transition from polythematic qasida to monothematic poem.

In Poem 12, the poet's focus is directed exclusively to the goshawk, who is glorified in military terminology, whereas Poem 13 adumbrates the narrative of the hunting expedition in which the poet rouses his huntsman or companions, leads the night expedition, and superintends the kill. All that is missing in the poem, in formal terms, is the commensal feast shared at the end of the hunt. As with Poem 12, the goshawk is the principal object of the poet's focus.

*

George Mackay Brown's "Hawk" breathes the same air of ferocity as the goshawk in these poems, even though Mackay Brown's raptor is shot over Bigging by "Jock."

Poems 14 to 21: Al-Shamardal ibn Sharīk

Al-Shamardal ibn Sharīk belonged to the Thaʿlabah ibn Yarbūʿ branch of Tamim. He was alive toward the end of the first Islamic century and into the early decades of the second, and, along with his brothers, participated in the wars of conquest in Khurāsān;

during this campaign, three of his brothers lost their lives. He died sometime after 109/727–28. His poetry on hunting themes was held in high esteem.

I have included all but one of the extant hunting poems and fragments ascribed to al-Shamardal, including one (Poem 16) that was included by al-Ṣūlī in his recension of the diwan of Abū Nuwās but omitted by al-Iṣbahānī in his recension. Ibn Ḥamdūn (495–562/1102–66) in the *Tadhkirah* quotes a version of the poem and attributes it to al-Shamardal. The fragment I omitted is almost identical to Poem 21, but for completeness I include it below.

All poems and fragments are composed in *mashṭūr al-rajaz* meter, one of the generic features of the developed tradition, and are replete with vocabulary that is today obscure and may have been intended to be arcane for the poet's original audiences. Consequently, much in my translation is conjectural.

Poem 14 in this selection is one of the earliest examples of the developed *ṭardiyyah*: it begins with the early-morning departure and moves into a description of a raptor that is probably the goshawk (based on a comparison of the description "falling / on her prey like a stone" with line 6 of Poem 12: "her attack, when cast, like a stone"). It describes the kill in hyperbolic fashion (a mythic eighty kills!), and concludes with a communal feast. For an alternative translation and brief discussion, see Stetkevych, *The Hunt*, 52–56.

Poem 16 is a further example of the developed *ṭardiyyah*, this time without the concluding communal feast: it ends with a vivid, brutal kill scene, reminiscent of ʿAbīd's Poem 2.

Unlike Poems 14 and 16, Poem 15 is not an example of the developed genre, but is rather a dynamic narrative of the poet's nocturnal battle against a marauding wolf that ends with an allusion to the wolf's possible death, pierced by the poet's arrow.

Fragments 17, 18, and 20 are treatments of specific raptor features, whereas fragments 19 and 21 are variations on the auroral scenes that open so many *ṭardiyyāt*.

There is an additional fragment, 21a, which is almost identical to 21, included in Seidensticker, *Die Gedichte des Šamardal*, 189 (§41):

Early, when the pink
of dawn shines
in the dark,
I go hunting.

*

The indomitability of al-Shamardal's goshawk in fragments 14 and 16 makes me think of Thom Gunn's "Tamer and Hawk" (1954), while the wolf's menace is akin to Randall Jarrell's "Snow Leopard" (1945), "the heart of heartlessness."

Poem 22: Abū l-Najm al-ʿIjlī: Harried by the Jinn

Abū l-Najm al-Faḍl (or al-Mufaḍḍal) ibn Qudāmah was widely recognized as one of the greatest *rajaz* poets of his generation. He was part of the court of the Umayyad caliph Hishām ibn ʿAbd al-Malik (r. 105–25/724–43) and dedicated panegyrics to the caliph, such as the petition of Poem 23, and to many of the Umayyad elites. The date of his death is not known, though we can presume that his five poems translated in this volume are of a later provenance than the compositions by Ḥumayd al-Arqaṭ, Ghaylān ibn Ḥurayth, and al-Shamardal ibn Sharīk.

The poet and the hunting expedition arrive at an abandoned water hole in the desert. After a torrential storm, the rains replenish the pool and attract a thirsty ostrich rooster whose feeding habits are described at length, with an almost linguistically antiquarian precision of detail for desert fauna and flora. The poem concludes with the poet's son Shaybān on horseback, killing this magnificent nonhuman.

The poem is an epic ostrich hunt. Because of the lexicographical cornucopia of Abū l-Najm's poem, many scholars have quoted sections and verses from it, so that it now exists as a series of disjointed fragments. I have rearranged these shards into as continuous a poem as I was able. Much in both my reconstruction and translation remains conjectural.

*

I find myself comparing the aesthetics of Abū l-Najm's nonhuman description with Marianne Moore's wonderful poem on the ostrich, "He 'Digesteth Harde Yron'" (1941).

Poem 23: Abū l-Najm al-ʿIjlī: Dyed Dark with Gore

This poem is a eulogistic petition addressed to the caliph Hishām ibn ʿAbd al-Malik (r. 105–25/724–43) in which the poet requests the caliph to restore or guarantee ancestral properties the poet is on the verge of losing, thus spelling doom for his family. The themes of the poem are subordinated to the overarching topic of the journey across perilous deserts to wait upon the caliph in his court. Gnomic advice offered to a daughter concerned for the poet's welfare frames the poet's supplication. The description of the camel, in which the mount is compared with an onager jack and an oryx bull, occurs *before* the poet leaves on his journey, rather than during the perilous journey, as so often in the pre-Islamic tradition. In this iteration of the oryx bull episode, the poet combines two of its key notions: the oryx's flight to safety, outstripping the dogs, and the oryx's battle with the dogs. In this figuration, the oryx, despite having outrun the salukis, decides to return to the fray and give battle. The resulting scene is unique.

*

The warrior ferocity of the oryx recalls Les Murray's "Pigs" (1993): "Us all fuckers then. And Big, huh? Tusked / the balls-biting dog and gutsed him wet." Unlike the victorious oryx, Murray's pigs end up "in no place with our heads upside down." Abū l-Najm's poem also bears comparison with John Davidson's "A Runnable Stag"

(1906), who, "with his hooves on fire, his horns like flame," is "not to be caught now, dead or alive."

Poem 24: Abū l-Najm al-ʿIjlī: Full of Bloodlust

This cheetah poem is extant in a series of quotations, fragments, and versions. As with Poem 22, I have rearranged these shards into as continuous a poem as possible, but much in both my reconstruction and my translation remains conjectural. The version that emerges from my reconstruction is a three-part qasida in *rajaz*: lines 1–2 have the air of the *nasīb* about them, while lines 48–49 appear to be part of a panegyric dedicated to a caliph or a member of the caliphal family. The patron of the poem was not a caliph if we go by the information provided by al-Iṣbahānī in *Aghānī*, 10:120, who introduces the poem as follows: "ʿAbd al-Malik ibn Bishr ibn Marwān instructed Abū l-Najm to describe his cheetahs." This is the earliest cheetah hunt poem extant and the only one on this subject contained in this selection.

After the arrival of the hunting expedition at its destination, the arrival of the cheetahs, conveyed on the rumps of horses, is described. They are managed by a cheetah handler who conducts the hunt. For all its pace and excitement, the description of the chase lacks some of the intensity that informs other chase scenes in this selection—Abū l-Najm creates a sense of distance and invites his audience to be spectators and observe what is probably a stage-managed hunt conducted in a paradise or game reserve.

There is some uncertainty over the attribution of the poem to Abū l-Najm. Al-Shimshāṭī, *Anwār*, 2:160–61, ascribes it to Abū Nuwās, and some of the verses of the poem are attributed to Ḥumayd al-Arqaṭ: see Hämeen-Anttila, *Dīwān of Abū'n-Nağm*, 17. Al-Iṣbahānī (Abū Nuwās, *Dīwān*, 2:324), corrects the misattribution to Abū Nuwās and ascribes the poem to Abū l-Najm.

*

The excitement that the poet and his audience feel at the power and dynamism of the cheetahs in action brings to mind Ted Hughes's indomitable "The Jaguar" (1957).

Poem 25: Abū l-Najm al-ʿIjlī: Coils Scraping on Coils

This long poem is the most extensively reconstructed of the five poems by Abū l-Najm included in this volume. Despite my restoration attempts, the resultant poem remains deficient: there are four verses I have been unable to incorporate into my version. My restoration basically adopts a qasida sequence of *nasīb*, oryx, and onager episodes, the latter featuring an indigent hunter in his wattle, and tribal boast (here most briefly cast as a wish for the annihilation of Tamīm). The second section of my reconstruction is a scene taken from camel pastoralism, perhaps a prelude to a storm description or a vehicle for the introduction of the description of the poet's camel. The onager hunt is memorable and repays comparison with Abū Dhu'ayb's poem (Poem 9) in this volume, with the added detail of the threat from the vipers that share the dugout with the hunter, a topic Abū l-Najm introduces regularly in his hunting scenes.

The presence in the poem of Abū l-Najm's contemporary Dhū l-Rummah (d. 117/735) looms large—as a poet, Dhū l-Rummah excelled at desert vignettes such as the onager hunt and oryx and ostrich scenes: for examples, see Schippers, "Animal Descriptions in Two *Qaṣīdahs* by Dhū l-Rummah: Some Remarks." In *Altarabische Dichtkunst*, 2:385–451, Thomas Bauer provides a magisterial study of Dhū l-Rummah's onager episodes. In fact, Dhū l-Rummah also employed the topic of the lair shared by a hunter with snakes: see Schippers, "Animal Descriptions," 204–5, and Bauer, *Altarabische Dichtkunst*, 406–16 (especially 411 and 413).

*

The hunter and snake bring to mind D. H. Lawrence's "Snake" (1921), his encounter with a snake at a watering trough in Taormina, Sicily. The poet is in awe of the snake's majesty and longs to engage with the creature: "Was it perversity, that I longed to talk to him? / Was it humility, to feel so honoured? / I felt so honoured."

Poem 26: Abū l-Najm al-ʿIjlī: The Hills Shimmered

My reconstruction of this poem incorporates the extant fragments to form a *nasīb* and a *raḥīl* with a camel description (no longer extant) that focuses on a classic comparison between camel and onager. I have reconstructed the onager episode along classic lines to include the blistering summer heat, the race to water, the hunter in his dugout with a bow and arrow (including Abū l-Najm's favored viper motif), and the successful hunt. Some of the features of the poem are unique—for example, the hunter is no longer indigent, but rather his wife has her hands full tending the pots in which the game is cooked; the hunter is scared of the viper that keeps him company; and Abū l-Najm interestingly devotes several verses to a description of the onager jenny.

*

Abū l-Najm's magnificent, albeit doomed, onagers contrast strongly with Samuel Taylor Coleridge's "To a Young Ass, Its Mother Being Tethered Near It" (1794), his utopian vision of pantisocracy: "Poor little Foal of an oppressed race!"

27: ʿAbd al-Ḥamīd al-Kātib: To the Beat of the Drums

Abū Yaḥyā (or Abū Ghālib) ʿAbd al-Ḥamīd al-Kātib ibn Yaḥyā ibn Saʿd al-ʿĀmirī, known as al-Kātib, "the State Bureaucrat," was educated in Kufa and gained employment in the central Umayyad administration in Damascus. He rose through the ranks to a position from which he would write official correspondence on behalf of the caliph Hishām ibn ʿAbd al-Malik (r. 105–25/724–43). In 114/732 he became amanuensis to Marwān ibn Muḥammad on the latter's appointment as governor of the province of Armenia and Azerbaijan. Marwān was appointed caliph in 127/745 and ʿAbd al-Ḥamīd assumed control of the Umayyad state apparatus. A devoted supporter of the Umayyad cause and his patron Marwān, ʿAbd al-Ḥamīd was killed in 132/750 by the Abbasids when they overthrew the Umayyad caliphate. Versions of about one hundred of his state and personal letters have survived, among the earliest extant examples of Arabic epistolography.

This epistle (*risālah*) addressed to the caliph, presumably Marwān ibn Muḥammad (though possibly Hishām ibn ʿAbd al-Malik), is the only such *risālah* to have survived on the topic of the hunt prior to its efflorescence many centuries later (see Jaako Hämeen-Anttila, *Maqama*, 213–15). It describes an elite hunting expedition in vivid detail and includes scenes in which hounds and raptors are used to run down gazelles; goshawks, peregrines, and sakers are flown at waterfowl; and mounted horsemen chase a herd of onagers, trapping them in a wooded valley—a rare instance in the corpus of an onager chase on horseback. The epistle is also remarkable for its description of the changing weather conditions the hunting party experienced. Throughout, ʿAbd al-Ḥamīd regularly attributes the hunting party's felicity and successes to God and His vicegerent the caliph.

In many ways, the epistle anticipates the long *rajaz* poem by Abū Firās (d. 357/968) on a successful day's hunt in Syria: see Montgomery, "Abū Firās's Veneric." It provides us with a rare insight into how the Umayyad hunting poem was shaped, developed, and transformed into the Abbasid *ṭardiyyah* several decades later. For the general context of the Umayyad hunt and its iconography, see Brey, "The Caliph's Prey"; Brey also provides an alternative edition and translation of ʿAbd al-Ḥamīd's *risālah* (262–67).

Parts of my translation remain conjectural. For "frustrated by the river" (Poem 1), all the MSS read *al-baḥr*, "the sea," so I have retained it, though ʿAbbās proposes *al-bahr*, "remoteness," or *al-buhr*, "breathlessness." The phrase "sorting them according to their condition" (Poem 4) is a conjectural translation for *maʿrifat aḥwālihā*, literally "knowledge of their conditions."

*

To my mind, the exultation ʿAbd al-Ḥamīd derives from the killing spree in the piece contrasts starkly with the clinical mundaneness of the guidance on how to package and handle "all offals" in Laurie Duggan's prose poem "Hearts" (1985): "Hearts are to be incised to enable them to be packed flat." And the militarism of the hunting complex is very much at variance with the sentiments expressed by Bertolt Brecht in "Der Kriegsgott" ("The God of War") (1949).

Glossary

This Glossary contains many names of places and plants. For place-names, the exact location of many of which is unclear, I have simply offered a general explanation, trying wherever possible to tie the place-name to the territory of the tribe with which it is associated. More information can be found in al-Bakrī's *Mustaʿjam mā staʿjama min asmāʾ al-bilād wa-l-mawāḍiʿ* and Thilo's indispensable *Die Ortsnamen in der altarabischen Poesie*. In many instances, the identification of flora is far from certain. I rely principally on Mandaville, *Flora of Eastern Saudi Arabia*.

Abū ʿAmr a brother of Ṣakhr al-Ghayy, killed by a snakebite; only known because of the poet's threnody (Poem 6).

Adam also Adām; a mountain in central Arabia.

ʿAmāyah a large mountain range in central Arabia.

ʿanam the red fruit of a shrub that grows in the Hijaz.

ʿĀnāt a place in southern Iraq, renowned for its wine.

arāk *Salvadora persica*, a shrub that grows in dense thickets on sand hummocks; its twigs were used as tooth sticks.

ʿArdah a place in the territory of Banū Saʿd ibn Thaʿlabah, a branch of Asad.

ʿarfaj *Rhanterium eppaposum*, a shrub grazed by livestock that grows in soft soil and is highly combustible when dried.

arṭā *Calligonum comosum*, also known as fire bush, an ascending shrub with white older branches and flexible green shoots, found in the deeper sands.

Asmā’ a woman’s name, common in the *nasīb* (amatory) section of a pre-Islamic qasida.

atḥamī a striped outer garment.

ayhuqān *Erucastrum arabicum*, a type of *Brassica*, an annual found in desert or dry shrublands..

bashām *Commiphora gileadensis*, the Arabian balsam tree.

Bathr a well in the territory of Hudhayl in Hijaz.

Bayḍah a place in the vicinity of Aleppo.

Bīshah a wadi in central Arabia.

Bujaylah Abū l-Najm al-ʿIjlī’s daughter.

Dakhūl a well in the vicinity of Wadi Duwāsir in Najd.

Dārat Juljul an oasis in central Arabia.

Ḍārij a water hole close to the northern dunes of the Qasīm.

Dārīn the main settlement of the island of Tārūt in the Persian Gulf, associated with the import of Indian goods.

darmā’ *Fagonia bruguieri*, a shrub with fragrant leaves.

Dawār an idol, possibly a baetyl, worshipped by circumambulation in pre-Islamic Arabia.

Dhanūb also al-Dhanā’ib; a small group of mountains in the territory of Asad.

Dhāt Firqayn a place in the territory of Asad.

Dhū l-ʿArjā’ a hill, possibly a water hole, in the territory of Muzaynah, in the vicinity of Nubāyiʿ (q.v.).

dhubaḥ an unidentified plant that is a favorite of ostriches.

Dhubyān ibn Baghīḍ ibn Rayth, a major kin group within Ghaṭafān.

eagle (Ar. liqwah, ʿuqāb) either *Hieraaetus fasciatus*, Bonelli’s eagle, or *Aquila heliaca*, the eastern imperial eagle. Bonelli’s eagle is pale and medium sized, while the eastern imperial eagle is dark and large. Bonelli’s eagle prefers to nest on cliff ledges. The eastern imperial nests in trees, but has been known to nest on cliffs. Both types of eagle prefer to still-hunt from perches, though the eastern imperial is less agile in the air than Bonelli’s eagle.

Falj a wadi stretching from the north of the Dahnā’ erg (sand sea) to Basra.

Fardah a mountain in northwestern Arabia.

Fāṭimah a woman Imru' al-Qays refers to as his lover.

Fayd an oasis in central Arabia, a station on the pilgrim route from Kufa to Mecca.

Fulayj a wadi connected to Falj (q.v.).

Ghawl a water hole in central Arabia.

Ghumaysā' a settlement in the territory of Kinānah.

goshawk (Ar. bāz) *Accipiter gentilis*, the northern goshawk, is a large and aggressive raptor; the female of the genus is noticeably larger than the male. When hunting, the goshawk will either hug the ground in flight or attack from a high soar.

Ḥajr also known as Ḥajr al-Yamāmah, a pre-Islamic settlement southeast of Riyadh.

ḥarshā' *Brassica tournefortii*, a desert annual known today as *ḥurayshā'*.

Ḥawmal a mountain ten miles (sixteen kilometers) southwest of Dakhūl in Najd.

ḥazā' *Deverra triradiata*, a aromatic shrub that is a favorite of camels.

Hijaz region in western Arabia in which Mecca and Medina are located.

Ḥimyar an important South Arabian kingdom that flourished from about the first century BC until most of South Arabia was overrun and occupied by the Ethiopian armies of Axum in the early sixth century AD.

Hishām ibn ʿAbd al-Malik Umayyad caliph who ruled from 105/724 to 125/743 and was patron of Abū l-Najm al-ʿIjlī.

houbara (Ar. ḥubārā) *Chlamydotis macqueenii*, MacQueen's bustard, a large bustard that nests in areas of dense scrub vegetation; when hunted, it rises into the air and spirals, in order to confuse the pursuer.

hullab *Euphorbia granulata*, "milkweed," a plant with a milky sap.

ḥuwwā'ah either *Picris babylonica*, an annual herb common in northern areas of the peninsula; *Launaea capitata*, a procumbent herb common in sandy and silty soil; *Launaea nuducaulis*, a perennial herb typically found in ravines and small wadis; or *Launaea prucumbens*, an herb more common to farmed areas than deserts.

hyena *Hyaena hyaena*, the striped hyena (not to be confused with the more famous spotted hyena), is a shy nocturnal scavenger that sports a bushy mane and lives largely off carrion.

ibex (Ar. waʿil) *Capra nubiana*, the Nubian ibex, is a species of goat that lives in mountainous areas. Ibex have long horns that grow up and then downward and backward. They are light brown with a white underbelly and white legs; the males have a dark dorsal stripe.

idmi (Ar. ādam) *Gazella gazella*, the mountain gazelle, a species that lives on mountain ridges and desert plateaus.

isḥil a type of tree, growing in similar soil as the *arāk* (q.v.), the twigs of which are used as tooth sticks.

Jāfil a famous Arabian horse.

Jafnah (r. AD 220–65) the first king of the Byzantine phylarchy later known as the Ghassanids.

Jahiliya term used to characterize the time before the advent of Islam, variously understood to mean the "time of ignorance (of Islam)" or the "time of barbarism."

jilbab a long and loose-fitting outer garment worn by women.

jiryāl a red plant dye.

Jumayrāt a place in the agricultural lands around Kufa.

kanahbul a type of acacia.

Khiyam also Khiyām, a mountain in southeastern Najd.

khuzāmā *Horwoodia dicksoniae*, an annual herb with violet flowers.

Kutayfah a mountain in central Arabia, part of the same chain as Mujaymir (q.v.).

Liwā a mountain in Tihāmah, in the territory of Banū Sulaym.

leveret (Ar. khuzaz) the young of the hare, presumably the desert hare (*Lepus capensis*) native to Arabia.

Mahrī a prized breed of camel from Mahrah, a region in Yemen.

Malham a settlement with a date-palm oasis northwest of Riyadh.

Malḥūb a water hole in the territory of Asad.

Ma'sal a rock massif in central Arabia, enclosing a narrow valley.

maysir a ritualized game of chance played with ten or eleven arrow shafts; the prize was a camel slaughtered and divided into ten parts (four thighs, four shins, and both shoulders).

Minā the towering massif of red granite in central Arabia.

Miqrāt a place in the Ḥazn plateau of northwestern Arabia.

Muḥajjar a mountain chain in central Arabia surrounded by sand flats.

Mujaymir a mountain in central Arabia, part of the same chain as Kutayfah (q.v.).

Murrah a subgroup of Ghaṭafān, and thus of Qays ʿAylān.

Musharraq either a fortification in the settlement of Hajar on the eastern seaboard of Arabia or (more plausibly for Abū Dhu'ayb's topography) the market of Taif.

nabʿ the wood of a shrub used for the manufacture of bows, possibly a species of *Grewia.*

Nawār an epithet ("reticent," "timid") used to describe the woman addressed by Labīd ibn Rabīʿah in his *Muʿallaqah.*

Nubāyiʿ a wadi in the territory of Muzaynah between Mecca and Medina.

onager (Ar. ḥimār waḥshī) *Equus hemionius hemippus*, the Syrian or Mesopotamian wild ass, an extinct subspecies that was native to Arabia; its coat changed from tawny brown in winter to pale yellow in summer. The onager, typically 660 pounds (300 kilos) in weight and six and a half feet (two meters) in length, was a proficient runner and could reach speeds of thirty-seven miles (sixty kilometers) per hour.

oryx (Ar. mahāh or baqar waḥshī) *Oryx leucoryx*, the Arabian oryx, a subspecies of antelope distinctive for its straight horns and white hide, black facial and caudal stripes, and dark-brown legs. Oryx are perfectly adapted to desert conditions and can go for long periods without water.

peregrine (Ar. shahīn) *Falco peregrinus brookei*, the peregrine falcon, a powerful raptor, agile in the air, with a distinctive stoop, at great speeds, on prey, often catching its prey in the air. Peregrines have dark mustache marks under each eye.

pin-tailed sandgrouse (Ar. qaṭāh) *Pterocles alchata*, a medium-sized bird that flies in flocks to water holes at dawn. Their eggs are laid in hollows the birds scrape out in open land. They bring water to their chicks by a technique known as "rocking," whereby the body is moved from side to side and the feathers are soaked in the water: the feathers trap the water, which is then carried back to the chicks.

Qafā Ḥibirr a mountain in the territory of Asad.

Qahr a chain of hills in central Arabia.

Qalīb a word meaning "well," apparently a place in the territory of Asad, possibly identical to Qulāb, a mountain in their territory.

Qanān a low-lying massif in central Arabia.

Qaṭan a mountain range with numerous water holes in central Arabia.

qullām unidentified plant.

Quryān unidentified place.

Quṣwān unidentified place.

Qutabiyyāt a mountain range or a water hole in the territory of Asad.

Rākis a place in the territory of Banū Saʿd ibn Thaʿlabah, a branch of Asad.

Rammān a complex of table mountains in central Arabia.

raqam a type of arrow, possibly decorated with geometric designs.

Rayyān a mountain in central Arabia, part of the Minā (q.v.) massif.

rhim (Ar. ri'm) *Gazella arabica*, an Arabian subspecies of the mountain gazelle.

Rijām an elongated mountain ridge in central Arabia with a water hole at its foot, in the same area as Ghawl and Minā (qq.v.).

Rukhām a mountain in the vicinity of Fardah (q.v.).

rukhāmā *Convulvulus cephalopodus*, a shrub with white roots and pink blossoms associated with the diet of onagers.

Sadīr a place in Iraq.

Ṣāʿidī epithet of arrows manufactured in a settlement in Yemen called Ṣaʿdah.

saker (Ar. ṣaqr) *Falco cherrug milvipes*, the eastern saker falcon, a large rufous-brown falcon that prefers to hunt from a vantage point and surprise its prey. It has excellent stamina and will tail-chase its prey until its prey is exhausted. Females are larger than males.

salaʿ unidentified plant.

Salmā a woman's name, common in the *nasīb* (amatory) section of a pre-Islamic qasida.

saluki (Ar. salūqī) a sight hound widely used by the Bedouin to hunt game, renowned for its stamina and speed over long distances.

Samāwah a desert between Kufa (or Mosul) and Syria, in the territory of Kalb.

Samharī epithet for a hard spear shaft, often explained as originally crafted by an individual named Samhar, who imported the shafts from India; also explained, more plausibly perhaps, as crafted in a village in Ethiopia.

sandgrouse see pin-tailed sandgrouse.

Ṣarīḥ a famous Arabian horse.

Sawā' an unidentified place, perhaps in the territory of Hudhayl in Hijaz.

sea onion (Ar. ʿunṣul) *Drimia maritima*, also known as squill or sea squill, is a plant that grows from a large bulb, often weighing as much as a kilo.

seeling the practice of sewing a raptor's eyelids shut, a method adopted by Middle Eastern falconers as part of training a bird.

Shābah a mountain in Hijaz, in the territory of Hudhayl.

Shaybān the son of Abū l-Najm al-ʿIjlī.

shīḥ *Artemisia sieberi*, an aromatic shrub whose smoke is used for medicinal purposes.

shihrī a grade horse, offspring of an Arabian dam and a non-Arabian sire.

Shurayf a plateau in central Arabia.

simʿ an unidentified predator, explained in the lexica as the offspring of a wolf and a hyena.

Sitār an extended, low-lying chain of hills in central Arabia.

Ṣuʿā'id a wadi that runs from southwest to northeast through central Arabia.

Ṣubāḥī a member of the clan Ṣubāḥ, a branch of Ḍabbah. The confederation they formed enjoyed a long alliance with Tamīm (q.v.).

Ṣunaybiʿāt water holes in the territory of Ghaṭafān.

suṭṭāḥ a member of the gourd family.

Ṣuwā'iq a place in Yemen.

Tabālah a wadi that connects with Bīshah (q.v.), and the site of a famous market in central Arabia.

Taghlam a place, possibly a water hole.

ṭaḥmā' *Suaeda vermiculata*, a shrub that grows in saline soil.

Tamīm a large and important lineage group.

Ṭams an unidentified place.

ṭarfāʾ a type of tamarisk.

Tawwaj an area west of Shiraz in Iran (where goshawks are said to come from) and a place in Hijaz where falcons are said to come from.

Taymāʾ a settlement in northwestern Arabia, on the edge of the Nefud desert.

Tazīdī an outer garment with red stripes.

thaghāmah *Stipagrostis plumose*, a perennial grass common in shallow sand.

Thaʿlab a tribesman of al-Muraqqish al-Akbar, apparently killed in the raid described in Poem 4.

Thalabūt a wadi in central Arabia.

Thabīr a mountain near Mecca.

Thuʿālibāt also Thuʿaylibāt and Thuʿayyalibāt; a place in the territory of Banū Saʿd ibn Thaʿlabah, a branch of Asad.

Tubbaʿ a dynastic title in Arabic for the dynasty that ruled southwestern Arabia between the third and sixth centuries AD.

Tūḍiḥ a place in the northern stretches of the Dahnāʾ erg (sand sea).

Ṭulkhām also possibly Ṭilḥām, a wadi in central Arabia.

Twin Mountains a mountain range in Najd controlled by Ṭayyiʾ, a powerful lineage group.

ʿUdhayb a water hole in the territory of Tamīm in Yamāmah.

Uḥāẓah a place in southern Arabia or a Ḥimyarite tribe (see Ḥimyar).

Umaymah a woman addressed by Abū Dhuʾayb.

Umm al-ʿAmr a woman Abū l-Najm al-ʿIjlī refers to as his beloved.

Umm Ḥuwayrith a woman Imruʾ al-Qays refers to as his lover.

Umm Rabāb a woman Imruʾ al-Qays refers to as his lover.

ʿUnayzah a woman Imruʾ al-Qays refers to as his lover.

Wajrah a steppe in central Arabia.

wars *Memecylon umbellatum*, a plant from whose leaves a yellow dye can be produced.

wolf (Ar. dhiʾb) *Canis lupus arabs*, a subspecies of gray wolf. It is small, adapted to the desert, and lives in small packs.

Yabrīn a desert with large sand dunes in the vicinity of the oasis of Yabrīn, lying east of the Dahnāʾ erg (sand sea).

Yadhbul a high massif in central Arabia.

yarak when a falcon or a hawk is described as being "in yarak," it is in a fit and proper condition for flying—that is, hunting.

Yazan a powerful clan from Ḥaḍramawt who in the sixth century dominated Ḥimyar (qv.).

ẓaby (1) the general term in Arabic for a gazelle, be it an idmi (q.v.) or a rhim (q.v.); (2) either a water hole in the territory of Banū Sulaym or a wadi in Tihāmah.

Bibliography

ʿAbbās, Iḥsān. *ʿAbd al-Ḥamīd ibn Yaḥyā al-Kātib wa-mā tabaqqā min rasāʾilihi wa-rasāʾil Sālim Abī l-ʿAlāʾ*. Amman: Dār al-Shurūq li-l-Nashr wa-l-Tawzīʿ, 1988.

ʿAbīd ibn al-Abraṣ. *Diwān ʿAbīd ibn al-Abraṣ*. Edited by Husayn Naṣṣār. Cairo: Sharikat Maktabat wa-Maṭbaʿat Muṣṭafā l-Bābī al-Ḥalabī wa-Awlādihi, 1957.

Abū D̲u'aib. *Neue Hudailiten-Diwane. Band I: Der Dīwān des Abū D̲u'aib*. Edited and translated by Joseph Hell. Hanover, Germany: Heinz Lafaire, 1926.

Abū l-Najm al-ʿIjlī. *Dīwān Abī l-Najm al-ʿIjlī*. Edited by Muḥammad Adīb ʿAbd al-Wāḥid Jumrān. Damascus: Maṭbūʿāt Majmaʿ al-Lughah al-ʿArabiyyah bi-Dimashq, 2006.

Abū Nuwās, al-Ḥasan ibn Hāniʾ. *Dīwān al-Ḥasan ibn Hāniʾ*. Bibliotheca Islamica 20b, vol. 2. Edited by Ewald Wagner. Wiesbaden, Germany: Franz Steiner, 1972.

———. *Dīwān Abī Nuwās bi-Riwāyat al-Ṣūlī*. Edited by Bahjat ʿAbd al-Ghafūr al-Ḥadīthī. Abu Dhabi: Dār al-Kutub al-Waṭaniyyah, 2010.

Allen, M. J. S., and G. R. Smith. "Some Notes on Hunting Techniques and Practices in the Arabian Peninsula." *Arabian Studies* 2 (1975): 108–47.

Allen, Mark. *Falconry in Arabia*. London: Orbis Books, 1984.

Allsen, Thomas T. *The Royal Hunt in Eurasian History*. Philadelphia: University of Pennsylvania Press, 2006.

ʿAntarah ibn Shaddād. *War Songs*. Translated by James E. Montgomery with Richard Sieburth. New York: New York University Press, 2018.

El-Ariss, Tarek. "Return of the Beast: From Pre-Islamic Ode to Contemporary Novel." *Journal of Arabic Literature* 47, nos. 1–2 (2016): 62–90.

Al-Bakrī. *Mustaʿjam mā staʿjama min asmāʾ al-bilād wa-l-mawāḍiʿ*. Edited by Muṣṭafā l-Saqqā. 4 vols. Cairo: Maṭbaʿat Lajnat al-Taʾlīf, 1945–51.

Al-Bāshā, ʿAbd al-Raḥmān. *Shiʿr al-ṭarad ilā nihāyat al-qarn al-thālith al-hijrī*. Beirut: Muʾassasat al-Risālah, 1974.

Bauer, Thomas. *Altarabische Dichtkunst: Eine Untersuchung ihrer Struktur und Entwicklung am Beispiel der Onagerepisode*. 2 vols. Wiesbaden, Germany: Harrassowitz, 1992.

———. "Muzarrids Qaṣīde vom reichen Ritter und den armen Jäger." In *Festschrift Ewald Wagner zum 65. Geburtstag. Band 2: Studien zur Arabischen Dichtung*, edited by Wolfhart Heinrichs and Gregor Schoeler, 42–71. Beirut: Franz Steiner Verlag, 1994.

———. "The Dawādār's Hunting Party: A Mamluk *Muzdawija Ṭardiyya*, probably by Shihāb al-Dīn Ibn Faḍl Allāh." In *O Ye Gentlemen: Arabic Studies on Science and Literary Culture in Honour of Remke Kruk*, edited by Arnoud Vrolijk and Jan P. Hogendijk, 291–312. Leiden, Netherlands: Brill, 2007.

Brey, Alexander. "The Caliph's Prey: Hunting in the Visual Cultures of the Umayyad Empire." PhD diss., Bryn Mawr, 2018.

Briggs, Kate. *This Little Art*. London: Fitzcarraldo Editions, 2017.

Dīwān al-Hudhaliyyīn. Edited by Aḥmad al-Zayn. Cairo: al-Dār al-Qawmiyyah li-l-Ṭibāʿah wa-l-Nashr, 1965.

Fahd, Toufic. "Nasr." *Encyclopaedia of Islam*. 2nd ed. Brill Online.

Farḥāt, Yūsuf Shukrī, ed. *Dīwān al-ṣaʿālīk*. Beirut: Dār al-Jīl, 1992.

Farrin, Raymond. *Abundance from the Desert: Classical Arabic Poetry*. Syracuse, NY: Syracuse University Press, 2010.

Gelder, G. J. H. van. *Beyond the Line: Classical Arabic Literary Critics on the Coherence and Unity of the Poem*. Leiden, Netherlands: Brill, 1982.

Goldziher, Ignaz. "Der Dîwân des Ġarwal b. Aus Al-Ḥuṭejʾa." *Zeitschrift der Deutschen Morgenländischen Gesellschaft* 46 (1892): 1–53, 173–225, 471–527; *Zeitschrift der Deutschen Morgenländischen Gesellschaft* 47 (1893): 43–87, 163–201.

Hämeen-Anttila, Jaako. *Dīwān of Abū'n-Nağm*. Materials for the Study of Rağaz Poetry, vol. 1. Helsinki: Studia Orientalia, 1993.

———. *Five Rağaz Collections*. Materials for the Study of Rağaz Poetry, vol. 2. Helsinki: Studia Orientalia, 1995.

———. *Minor Rağaz Collections*. Materials for the Study of Rağaz Poetry, vol. 3. Helsinki: Studia Orientalia, 1996.

———. *Maqama: A History of a Genre (Diskurs der Arabistik, 5)*. Wiesbaden, Germany: Harrassowitz, 2002.

Ḥmēdān al-Shwēʿir. *Arabian Satire: Poetry from 18th-Century Najd*. Edited and translated by Marcel Kurpershoek. New York: New York University Press, 2017.

Hollander, John, ed. *Animal Poems*. London: Everyman, 1994.

Hughes, Ted. *Poetry in the Making*. London: Faber and Faber, 1967.

Hussein, Ali Ahmad. "Two Sources for Abu Dhu'ayb al-Hudhali's Famous Elegy." *International Journal of Middle East Studies* 53 (2021): 213–33.

Al-Ḥuṭay'ah. *Dīwān al-Ḥuṭay'ah bi-sharḥ Ibn al-Sikkīt wa-l-Sukkarī wa-l-Sijistānī*. Edited by Nuʿmān Amīn Ṭāhā. Cairo: Sharikat Maktabat wa-Maṭbaʿat Muṣṭafā l-Bābī al-Ḥalabī wa-Awlādihi, 1958.

———. *Dīwān al-Ḥuṭay'ah bi-sharḥ wa-riwāyat Ibn al-Sikkīt*. Edited by Mufīd Muḥammad Qamīḥah. Beirut: Dār al-Kutub al-ʿIlmiyyah, 1993.

Ibn Ḥamdūn, Muḥammad ibn al-Ḥasan. *Al-Tadhkirah al-Ḥamdūniyyah*. Edited by Iḥsān ʿAbbās and Bakr ʿAbbās. 10 vols. Beirut: Dār Ṣādir, 1996.

Ibn Maymūn, Muḥammad ibn al-Mubārak. *Muntahā l-ṭalab min ashʿār al-ʿArab: The Utmost in the Search for Arab Poetry*. Edited by Fuat Sezgin. 3 vols. Frankfurt am Main: Institute for the History of Arabic-Islamic Science at the Johann Wolfgang Goethe University, 1986–93.

———. *Muntahā l-ṭalab min ashʿār al-ʿArab*. Edited by Mohamed Nabil Ṭuraifi. 9 vols. Beirut: Dār Ṣādir, 1999.

Al-Iṣbahānī, Abū l-Faraj. *Kitāb al-Aghānī l-kabīr*. Edited by Iḥsān ʿAbbās, Ibrāhīm al-Saʿāfīn, and Bakr ʿAbbās. 25 vols. Beirut: Dār Ṣādir, 2008.

Al-Jāḥiẓ, Abū ʿUthmān. *Kitāb al-Bayān wa-l-tabyīn*. Edited by ʿAbd al-Salām Muḥammad Hārun. 4 vols. Cairo: Maktabat al-Khānjī, 1948–50.

Jamil, Nadia. *Ethics and Poetry in Sixth-Century Arabia*. Oxford: Gibb Memorial Trust, 2017.

Jones, Alan. *Early Arabic Poetry*. Vol. 1, *Marāthī and Ṣuʿlūk Poems*. Reading, UK: Ithaca Press, 1992.

———. *Early Arabic Poetry*. Vol. 2, *Select Odes*. Reading, UK: Ithaca Press, 1999.

Kosegarten, Johann. *Carmina Hudsailitarum*. London: The Oriental Translation Fund, 1854.

Kushājim, Maḥmūd ibn al-Ḥusayn. *Al-Maṣāyid wa-l-maṭārid*. Edited by Muḥammad Riḍwān ʿAdnān Dāwūdī and ʿĀrif ʿAbd al-Aḥmad ʿAbd al-Ghanī. Damascus: Dār Saʿd al-Dīn wa-Dār Kinān, 2016.

Labīd ibn Rabīʿah. *Dīwān Labīd ibn Rabīʿah al-ʿĀmirī*. Edited by Iḥsān ʿAbbās. Kuwait: al-Turāth al-ʿArabī, 1962.

———. *Dīwān Labīd ibn Rabīʿah: Sharḥ al-Ṭūsī*. Edited by Ḥannā Naṣr Ḥittī. Beirut: Dār al-Kitāb al-ʿArabī, 1993.

Al-Lāmiyyatān. Edited by ʿAbd al-Muʿīn al-Mallūḥī. Damascus: Wizārat al-Thaqāfah wa-l-Irshād al-Qawmī, 1966.

Larsen, David. "The *Muʿallaqah* of ʿAbīd ibn al-Abraṣ: Meditations on Life." In *The Muʿallaqāt for Millennials*, 460–489. Dahran, Saudi Arabia: King Abdulaziz Center for World Culture, 2020.

Lyall, Charles James, ed. and trans. *The Dīwāns of ʿAbīd ibn al-Abraṣ of Asad and ʿĀmir ibn al-Ṭufail, of ʿĀmir ibn Ṣaʿṣāʿah*. Cambridge, UK: Gibb Memorial, 1980.

———. *The Mufaḍḍalīyāt: An Anthology of Ancient Arabian Odes*. 2 vols. London: Oxford University Press, 1918–20.

Macdonald, Helen. *H is for Hawk*. London: Vintage, 2014.

Mandaville, James P. *The Flora of Eastern Saudi Arabia*. London: Routledge, 2016.

Marvin, William. "Medieval Blood Sport." In *Animals, Animality and Literature*, edited by Bruce Boehrer and Molly Hand, 57–72. Cambridge: Cambridge University Press, 2018.

Al-Marzūqī, Abū ʿAlī Aḥmad ibn Muḥammad. *Sharḥ dīwān al-Ḥamāsah li-Abī Tammām*. Edited by Gharīd al-Shaykh. 4 vols. Beirut: Dār al-Kutub al-ʿIlmiyyah, 2002.

Al-Māyidī ibn Ẓāhir. *Love, Death, Fame: Poetry and Lore from the Emirati Oral Tradition.* Edited and translated by Marcel Kurpershoek. New York: New York University Press, 2022.

Miller, Nathaniel. "Tribal Poetics in Early Arabic Culture: The Case of Ashʿār al-Hudhaliyyīn." PhD diss., University of Chicago, 2016.

Montgomery, James Edward. "Dichotomy in *Jāhilī* Poetry." *Journal of Arabic Literature* 17 (1986): 1–20.

———. "Abū Firās's Veneric *Urjūzah Muzdawijah.*" *Middle Eastern Literatures* 2, no. 1 (1999): 61–74.

The Muʿallaqāt for Millennials: Pre-Islamic Arabic Golden Odes. Dhahran, Saudi Arabia: King Abdulaziz Center for World Culture (Ithra), 2020.

Al-Muzarrid ibn Ḍirār. *Dīwān al-Muzarrid ibn Ḍirār al-Ghaṭafānī.* Edited by Khalīl Ibrāhīm al-ʿAṭiyyah. Baghdad: Maṭbaʿat Asʿad, 1962.

Oswald, Alice. *Memorial.* London: Faber, 2011.

Ruymbeke, Christine van. "Sir William Jones and the Anvar-e Sohayli: With a Fortuitous but Nevertheless Essential Note on the Orient Pearls." In *From Asl to Zaʾid: Essays in Honour of Eva M. Jeremias*, edited by I. Szanto, 221–38. Piliscsaba, Hungary: The Avicenna Institute of Middle Eastern Studies, 2015.

Al-Ṣāliḥī, ʿAbbās Muṣṭafā. *Al-Ṣayd wa-l-ṭarad fī al-shiʿr al-ʿarabī ḥattā nihāyat al-qarn al-thānī l-hijrī.* Baghdad: Maṭbaʿat Dār al-Salām, 1974.

Schippers, Arie. "Animal Descriptions in Two *Qaṣīdahs* by Dhū l-Rummah: Some Remarks." *Journal of Arabic Literature* 23, no. 3 (1992): 191–207.

Seidensticker, Tilman. *Die Gedichte des Šamardal ibn Šarīk.* Wiesbaden, Germany: Harrassowitz, 1983.

———. "Ṭardiyya." *Encyclopaedia of Islam.* 2nd ed. Brill Online.

Al-Shimshāṭī, Abū l-Ḥasan ʿAlī ibn Muḥammad. *Kitāb al-Anwār wa-maḥāsin al-ashʿār.* Edited by al-Sayyid Muḥammad Yūsuf. 2 vols. Kuwait: Maṭbaʿat Ḥukūmat Kuwayt, 1977.

Simms, Colin. *Goshawk Poems.* Bristol, UK: Shearsman Books, 2017.

Smith, G. Rex. "Hunting Poetry (*Ṭardiyyāt*)." In *ʿAbbasid Belles Lettres (The Cambridge History of Arabic Literature)*, edited by Julia

Ashtiany, T. M. Johnstone, J. D. Latham, and R. B. Serjeant, 167–84. Cambridge: Cambridge University Press, 1990.

Stetkevych, Jaroslav. *The Hunt in Arabic Poetry: From Heroic to Lyric to Metapoetic*. Notre Dame, IN: University of Notre Dame Press, 2016.

———. "The ʿAyniyyah of Abū Dhuʾayb al-Hudhalī: The Achievement of a Classical Allegorical Form." *Journal of Arabic Literature* 51 (2020): 273–324.

Stetkevych, Suzanne. *The Mute Immortals Speak: Pre-Islamic Poetry and the Poetics of Ritual*. Ithaca, NY: Cornell University Press, 1993.

Stetkevych, Suzanne, and Khalid Stetkevych. "The *Muʿallaqah* of Imruʾ al-Qays: Adventures of Youthful Passion." In *The Muʿallaqāt for Millennials*, 24–89. Dahran, Saudi Arabia: King Abdulaziz Center for World Culture, 2020.

———. "The *Muʿallaqah* of Labīd ibn Rabīʿah: The Mute Immortals." In *The Muʿallaqāt for Millennials*, 207–51. Dahran, Saudi Arabia: King Abdulaziz Center for World Culture, 2020.

Al-Sukkarī, Abū Saʿīd al-Ḥasan. *Kitāb Sharḥ ashʿār al-Hudhaliyyīn*. Edited by ʿAbd al-Sattār Aḥmad Farrāj. 2 vols. Cairo: Maṭbaʿat al-Madanī, n.d.

Thilo, Ulrich. *Die Ortsnamen in der altarabischen Poesie*. Wiesbaden, Germany: Harrassowitz, 1958.

Al-Tibrīzī, Abū Zakariyyā Yaḥyā ibn ʿAlī. *Sharḥ al-qaṣāʾid al-ʿashr*. Edited by Fakhr al-Dīn Qabāwah. Beirut: Dār al-Āfāq al-Jadīdah, 1980.

———. *Sharḥ Dīwān al-Ḥamāsah li-Abī Tammām*. Edited by Gharīd al-Shaykh. 2 vols. Beirut: Dār al-Kutub al-ʿIlmiyyah, 2000.

Al-ʿUkbarī, Abū l-Baqāʾ. *Iʿrāb lāmiyyat al-ʿArab*. Edited by Muḥammad Adīb ʿAbd al-Wāḥid Jumrān. Beirut: al-Maktab al-Islāmī, 1988.

Wagner, Ewald. *Grundzüge der klassischen arabischen Dichtung. Band II: Die arabische Dichtung in islamischer Zeit*. Darmstadt: Wissenschaftliche Buchgesellschaft, 1988.

Weipert, Reinhart. "Abū n-Naǧm al-Iǧlī—eine Nachlese." *Zeitschrift der Deutschen Morgenländischen Gesellschaft* 149, no. 1 (1999): 1–78.

White, T. H. *The Goshawk*. London: Weidenfeld and Nicholson, 2015.

Al-Zamakhsharī, Maḥmūd ibn ʿUmar. *Kitāb Aʿjab al-ʿajab fī lāmiyyat al-ʿArab*. Cairo: n. p., n. d.

Further Reading

Ahsan, Muhammad M. *Social Life under the Abbasids*. London: Longman, 1979.

Almond, Richard. *Medieval Hunting*. Stroud, UK: The History Press, 2011.

Armitage, Simon, and Tim Dee, eds. *The Poetry of Birds*. London: Viking, 2009.

Bodio, Stephen J. *The Hounds of Heaven: Living and Hunting with an Ancient Breed*. New York, NY: Skyhorse Publishing, 2016.

Burnett, Charles, and Baudouin van den Abeele, eds. *Falconry in the Mediterranean Context during the Pre-Modern Era*. Bibliotheca Cynegetica, vol. 9. Geneva: Librairie Droz, 2021.

Clark, William S. *A Field Guide to the Raptors of Europe, the Middle East, and North Africa*. Oxford: Oxford University Press, 1999.

Cummins, John. *The Hound and the Hawk: The Art of Medieval Hunting*. London: Weidenfeld and Nicolson, 1988.

Maraqten, Mohammed. "Hunting in Pre-Islamic Arabia in Light of the Epigraphic Evidence." *Arabian Archaeology and Epigraphy* 26 (2015): 208–34.

Muldoon, Paul, ed. *The Faber Book of Beasts*. London: Faber and Faber, 1997.

Oswald, Alice, ed. *A Ted Hughes Bestiary: Poems*. London: Faber and Faber, 2014.

Steel, Karl. *How to Make a Human: Animals and Violence in the Middle Ages*. Columbus: The Ohio State University Press, 2011.

Stetkevych, Jaroslav. "Name and Epithet: The Philology and Semiotics of Animal Nomenclature in Early Arabic Poetry." *Journal of Near Eastern Studies* 45, no. 2 (1986): 89–124.

Index

ʿAbbās, Iḥsān, 107
ʿAbd al-Ḥamīd al-Kātib: life of, 106–107; prose epistle of, xiii, xxviii, xxxi, xxxiii, 74–77, 106–108
ʿAbīd ibn al-Abraṣ: life of, 82; qasidas of, 8–13, 82–84
Abū ʿAmr, xviii, 21–22
Abu Dhabi Falcon Hospital, xiii, xxxiv
Abū Dhu'ayb, Khuwaylid ibn Khālid: life of, 94–95; qasida of, xxv, 34–37, 90, 94–96, 105
Abū Firās al-Ḥamdānī, xxxii, xxxiii, 107
Abū l-Muthallam, 90
Abū l-Najm al-ʿIjlī: life of, 102; misattribution of poems to, 98, 104; qasidas of, xxviii, 53–73, 94, 102–106
Abū Nuwās: *Dīwān* of, 99, 100, 101, 104; misattribution of poems to, 99–100, 104; mention of, xiii, xxxii, xxxiii, 99, 100, 101
Abū Tammām, 99
acacias, 3, 22
Adam (mountains), 14
ʿAmāyah (mountains), xxiv, 14
ambergris, 65
al-Amīn, Caliph, xxx
ʿAmr ibn Qamī'ah, 85
amulets, 4, 21. *See also* charms
ʿanam (fruit), 14
ʿĀnāt, 10
Anglo-Saxon poetry, 94
anxiety, 80, 90
arāk (shrub), 70
ʿArdah, 8
arenas, 6
ʿarfaj (shrub), 25
armies, 5, 15–16, 79
armor, 19, 27, 32, 93, 95
arrows: hunting with bows and, xxv, xxviii, xxx, xxxi, xl, 101, 106; in poems' texts, xv, xxv, 17, 18, 19, 22, 25, 26, 27, 30, 31, 33, 35, 36, 39, 45, 68, 72, 73, 96
arṭā (shrub), 19, 36, 59
al-Aʿshā Maymūn ibn Qays, 85
Asmā', 14, 72, 85
assegai, 43–44
athamī (garment), 20
ayhuqān (*Brassica* type), 23

Bakr ibn Wā'il (tribe), xxiv, 84
Barthes, Roland, xxvi
bashām (tree), 21
basīṭ meter, 83

Bathr, 35
battles/battlefields, xxiv, 6, 19, 26, 27, 29, 31, 32, 41, 80, 82, 83, 85, 93, 95, 96, 101, 103
Bayḍah, 71
bāz (goshawk). *See* goshawks (*bāz*)
bees, 18, 89
birds, xviii, xxvii, xxxi, xxxiv–xxxv, xlivn15, 6, 10, 22, 40, 44, 53, 56, 74–76, 89, 99. *See also under names of specific birds*
Bīshah (wadi), 24
Bishop, Elizabeth, 91
Bishr ibn ʿAmr, 85
blood, xix, 6, 26, 30, 35, 36, 39, 44, 56, 60, 62, 63–64, 68, 73, 87
blood vengeance, 62, 86, 89, 92
bloodwite, 27
boasting, 4, 17, 80, 83, 88, 91, 93–94, 105
body chains, 4
bone dice, 19, 89
Bonelli's eagles (*laqwah*), xxviii
The Book of Taliesin, 94
bows: efficacy of, 88; hunting with arrows and, xxviii, xxx, xxxi, xl; in poems' texts, 17, 19, 33, 35, 68–69, 72, 75, 88, 106
bread, 38
Brecht, Bertolt, 108
bromegrass, 71
Bujaylah, 57
burkah (teals), xxix
bustards. *See* houbaras

caliphate, 62, 93, 107
caliphs, xxx, xxxiii, xliiin10, 64, 93, 95, 97, 98, 102–104, 106–107. *See also under names of specific caliphs*
calligraphy, 14
camels: descriptions of, 10, 24–26, 59, 60–62, 82, 91, 103, 105, 106; in poems' texts, 3, 5, 7, 9, 10, 12, 16, 17–19, 24–26, 27, 30, 35, 36, 46, 53, 56, 58, 59, 60–62, 63, 65, 67, 70, 71, 72, 80; sacrificing of, 80
candles, 31
Canopus, 35
care, xxxiv, xxxv, 5, 19, 28, 30, 60, 88
carrion, 18
cauldrons, 6, 28
chain mail, xvi, 28, 36, 46
charms, 21, 34 *See also* amulets
cheetahs, xxiii, xxviii, xxviii, xxx, 63, 99, 104–105,
children, 4, 5, 6, 9, 17, 20, 39, 57, 58, 88
chukars, xxx
Clare, John, 89
Clarke, Gillian, 98
cloaks, xv, xvii, 4, 21, 33, 35, 40, 53, 71
clouds, 7, 12, 21, 23, 24, 25, 35, 53, 55, 56, 59, 71, 75
cloves, 3
cockcrows, 26
Coleridge, Samuel Taylor, 106
cooks/cooking, 7, 106
corpses, xxiv, 14, 25
coverts, 21, 61, 74, 75
crimes, xl, 19, 88, 89
crows, 21, 22, 57
curtains, 24

Dakhūl (wadi), 3
Dārat Juljul, 3
Ḍārij (water hole), 7
Dārīn, 65
darmāʾ (shrub), 54

dates/date palms, xviii, 5, 7, 8, 14, 22, 25, 27, 30, 58, 66, 70
David, 37
Davidson, John, 103
Dawār, 6
dawn, 5, 7, 10, 19, 22, 23, 36, 40, 50, 52, 64, 75, 102
Death: Fate and, xviii, xxiii, xxiv, xxv; in poems' texts, 8–9, 15, 21, 26, 29, 33, 34, 35, 46, 57, 58, 64, 68, 70; mentions of, xviii, xix
debris, 7, 53
Dhanūb (mountains), 8
Dharker, Imtiaz, 84
Dhāt Firqayn, 8
Dhū l-ʿArjāʾ (water hole), 35
Dhū l-Rummah, xxxix, 105
dhubaḥ (plant), 55
Dhubyān, xxxvi, 29, 93
dice, 19, 89
dinars, 14
does, 4, 6, 24, 25, 29, 89, 91–92
dogs, xix, xxvii, xxviii, xxx, xxxi, 20, 26, 33, 36, 53, 59, 60, 68, 74, 75, 92, 95, 99, 103. *See also* salukis; sheepdogs
drums, 74, 76, 77
ducks, xxx
Duggan, Laurie, 108
dust, xvii, xix, xxxiv, 19, 25, 42, 43, 45, 46, 55, 56, 64, 71, 75
Dyer, John, 92

eagles, xviii, xix, xxv, xxviii, xliiin7, 8–11, 13, 22, 82–83, 90, 95, 99. *See also* Bonelli's eagles
earrings, xv, 36, 65, 96
east wind, 59
Edson, Russel, 94
eggs, 4, 5, 12, 29, 55, 59
enjambment, xli, xlii
Euphrates, xxxvii, 70

fakhr (tribal boasts), 80, 91. *See also* boasting
falconers, xxx, xliiin1, 42
falconry/hawking, xxviii, xxx, xxxi, xxxiv, xliiin10
falcons, xiii, xxiii, xxviii, xxx, xxxiii, xxxiv–xxxv, xliiin1, 20, 42, 99. *See also* peregrine falcons; saker falcons
Falj (wadi), 61
fame, xxiv, xxv, 29, 31, 32, 33, 37, 79, 83, 93
famines, 13, 15, 28, 58
Fardah, 24
fat, 3, 36, 39, 70, 96
Fate: depredations of, xxiii, 82–83, 94–95; in hunting complex, xxvi, xxiii, 90; inexorability of, xvii–xviii, xxiii–xxvi, 82–83, 90; in poems' texts, 8, 9, 14, 15, 19, 21, 22, 25, 26, 34–37, 57–58, 61, 62, 68
Fāṭimah, 4, 5, 80
fawns, 4, 22, 24, 31, 62, 92
Fayd, 24
feasts/feasting, xxxii, xxxv, 28, 30, 36, 39, 44, 55, 56, 81, 98, 100, 101
feathers, xvii, xxxiv, 9, 40, 54, 55, 56, 61, 72
fevers, xvi, 19, 46
fifes, 30
fires, 20, 25, 27, 44, 50, 59, 71, 104,
firewood, xvii, xix, 46
firing (of weapon), xviii, xx, xxv, 17, 22, 36, 39, 45, 47, 56, 69, 97. *See also* arrows; bows

fishes, xvi, 12, 31
flocks, 45, 88
floods/flooding, 7, 8, 10, 12, 29–33, 53–54, 81, 84, 93–94
flowers, 55, 60, 71, 75
foals/foaling, 24, 31, 35, 36, 39, 96, 106
food, xx, xxxi, 13, 17, 18, 22, 38, 84
foxes, 6, 10–11, 75, 83
friendships, 9, 24, 33
fruits, xvii, xxv, xxxv, 4, 5, 21, 66
Fulayj (wadi), 61
gazelles, xxix, 23, 61, 75, 90, 107
geese (*iwazz*), xxx
gems, 4

Ghawl (water hole), 23
Ghaylān ibn Ḥurayth: life of, 99; qasidas of, 41–42, 99–100, 102
al-Ghayy, Ṣakhr: life of, 90; qasida of, xxiv, 21–22, 90–91
glory, xxv, 37, 59, 86, 91–92, 95
God: in epistle, 74–77; Fate and, xxiii; hunting party's successes and, 98, 107; in poems' texts, 4, 9, 13, 16, 21, 45, 57–58
The Gododdin, 96
gold, 62
gore, 35, 42, 56, 57–62, 76, 103
goshawks (*bāz*), xi, xvi, xxviii, xxix, xxxi, xxxiii, xxxv, 30, 76, 99–100, 101, 102, 107
gourds, 3, 6, 15
grasses, xx, 23, 29, 35, 54, 59, 66, 71, 75, 83
grouse, 9, 12, 19, 20, 27, 31, 61, 88, 89. *See also* sandgrouse
Gunn, Thom, 102
Hafez, xli
hair, xx, 5, 6, 8, 18, 20, 29, 30, 33, 56, 58, 88
hairpins, 26
al-Ḥajjāj ibn Yūsuf, 98
Ḥajr, xxiv, 64, 85
Ḥamāsah, 98
Hämeen-Anttila, Jaako, xilvn13, 99–100, 104, 107
harems, xxv, 35, 58, 66, 71, 76, 95
hares, xviii, xix, xxix, 22, 43, 44, 75
ḥarshāʾ (plant), 55
harvests, 27, 70
hauberks, 28, 37
hawks, xi, xvi, xvii, xix, xxviii, xxix, xxxi, xxxiii, xxxv, 30, 76, 99–100, 101, 102, 107. *See also* goshawks; sparrow hawks
Ḥawmal, 3
ḥazāʾ, 55
Hearnes, Vicky, 92
hearths, 53
hearts, xviii, xxv, 4, 5, 9, 10, 14, 17, 18, 19, 22, 29, 41, 42, 43, 45, 53, 62, 63, 88, 102, 108
henna, 6, 29
herds, xl, 6, 17, 23, 25, 29, 35, 39, 40, 66, 68, 71, 73, 75, 81, 88, 107
hideouts, 68, 72
hijabs (garment), 41, 43, 50
Hishām ibn ʿAbd al-Malik, caliph, xxxiii, 102, 103, 106, 107
Holes, Clive, xiii, xxxv
honor, xxv, 13, 16, 28, 32, 39, 84, 88, 93
hoppers, 54
horns (of animals), xxix, 20, 21, 26, 36, 60, 66, 72, 92, 104
horses: in general, xv, xix, xviii, xxx, 81, 82, 83, 92, 93, 96, 98–99, 102,

104, 107; association with water, 6–7, 30, 81; compared to raptors, 40, 82–83, 99; in epistle, 75–77; in poems' texts, 6–7, 27, 30, 37, 40, 56, 58, 63
hospitality, 97, 98
houbaras, xvii, xix, xxix, xxxiv, 41, 42, 44, 46, 63
howdahs, 3, 23
Hughes, Ted, xi, xvii, 82, 89, 99, 105
Ḥumayd al-Arqaṭ: life of, 98; misattribution of poems to, 104; qasida of, 40, 98–99, 102
hunted/prey, xvii–xviii. *See also under specific prey animals*
hunting: in general, xxiii–xxxvi; of nonhuman hunted, xxix–xxx; by nonhuman hunters, xxvii–xxviii; royal, xxxi–xxxii; subsistence, xxxi–xxxii; terrain of, xxix. *See also* hunting complex; huntsmen
hunting complex: in general, xxiii–xxvii, xxxii, xxxv, xxxix, xl, 90, 98; blood vengeance in, 89; Fate in, xxvi, 90; God in, 98, 107; humans/nonhumans in, xxvi–xxvii; militarism and, 108. *See also ṭardiyyah*
hunting instincts, xxvi–xxvii
huntsmen: in general, xxiii, xxx; consciousness of experience of animals, xxvi, xxxvi, 92; in poems' texts, 63, 64, 100; starving, 33, 58, 94
al-Ḥuṭay'ah: life of, 97; qasida of, xxxii, 38–39, 97–98
ḥuwwā'ah (herb), 55
hyenas, 7, 17, 20, 88
hyper-focus, powers of, xxvii
hypotaxis, xli

ibexes: xv, xvii, xviii, xx, 88–89; circumambulation by, 88; deaths of, xix, xxiv–xxv, 85–86, 90, 95; grandeur of, 90; in poems' texts, 7, 14, 20, 21–22, 37
ibises, xxx
Ibn al-Anbārī, 93
Ibn Ḥamdūn, 101
Ibn al-Muʿtazz, xxxii, xxxiii
Ibn al-Zubayr, 98
Imru' al-Qays ibn Ḥujr: life of, 79; qasida of, xlii, 3–7, 79–82
invectives, 33, 93, 97, 98
al-Iṣbahānī, Ḥamzah, 99–101, 104
isḥil (tree), 5
iwazz (geese), xxx

Jāfil, 31
Jafnah, 15, 86
Jahiliya, xxiii, xxxii–xxxiii, 80, 82, 83, 87, 93
al-Jāḥiẓ, xxxiv
Jarrell, Randall, 102
Jarwal ibn Aws. *See* al-Ḥuṭay'ah
Jaz' ibn Ḍirār, 93
jilbab (garment), 50
jinns, xxi, 20, 27, 53–56, 61, 70, 102
jiryāl (dye), 70
Jones, Alan, 96
judges, xxv, 21, 31
Jumada, 24
Jumayrāt, 63

al-Kātib, ʿAbd al-Ḥamīd. *See* ʿAbd al-Ḥamīd al-Kātib
Khiyam, xxiv, 14

kin, xxv, 9, 15, 17, 62, 87–88
knights, 28, 29, 93
knives, xxv, 22, 41
Kushājim, Maḥmūd ibn al-Ḥusayn, 100
Kutayfah (mountains), 7

Labīd ibn Rabīʿah: life of, 91; qasida of, 23–28, 91–92
laments, xvi, xxiv, xxxv, xlivn15, 18, 85, 94, 95
lamps, 5, 7, 31, 37, 84
lances, 30
landslides, 6
laqwah (Bonelli's eagle), xxviii
larks, 7, 18, 54
Lawrence, D. H., 92, 105
Leaves of Grass, 83
leverets, 49. *See also* hares
Levertov, Denise, 91
Lewis, Gwyneth, 94
lightning, 7, 12, 59, 84
lions, xix, xx, 7
litters, 14, 33, 80, 85
Liwā (mountains), 72
locusts, 73, 75
looking glasses, 4
Lowell, Amy, 84
lutes, 26
Lyall, Charles James, 83, 84, 86

MacDiarmid, Hugh, 98
Macdonald, Helen, xiii, xxxv, xlivn16
MacQueen's bustards. *See* houbaras
Mahrī (camel breed), 58, 60
Malham, 14
Malḥūb (water hole), 8, 43
mallard, xxix
marthiyahs (threnodies), xvi, xxiii–xxv, 91, 95
Marvin, William, xxvi, xxvii
Marwān II, caliph, xxxiii
Ma'sal (mountains), 3
mashṭūr al-rajaz meter, xlii, 98, 101
al-Māyidī ibn Ẓāhir, 84
maysir (game of chance), 27
meters: in general, xli; *basīṭ*, 83; *mashṭūr al-rajaz*, xlii, 98, 101; *rajaz*, xxxiii; *sarīʿ*, 85–86
midday, 19, 26, 61, 71
milk, 36, 58, 66, 96
mills, 49
millstones, 67, 72
Minā (mountains), 23, 87
mirages, xxi, 20, 43
mist, 75
moles (birthmarks), 32
monks, 5, 7, 23, 31
Montague, John, 84
moon, 17, 32
Moore, Marion, 103
mortar, 6
mountain pools, 67
mountain retreats/homes, 17, 20, 21
mountains, xvi, xx, xxix, 12, 17, 20, 21, 24, 61, 67, 71, 75, 87, 88, 89. *See also under names of specific mountain ranges*
Muʿallaqāt ("The Suspended Odes"), xxiv, 79, 82, 85, 91
The *Mufaḍḍalīyyāt*, 86, 96
Muḥajjar (mountains), 24
Mujaymir (mountains), 7
Muldoon, Paul, 89
al-Muraqqish al-Akbar: family of, xxiv, 84–85; life of, xxiv, 84–85; qasida of, xxiv, 14–16, 84–86, 90
al-Muraqqish al-Aṣghar, 85
Murrah, 24

Murray, Les, 103
Musharraq, 34, 96
musk, 3, 5, 14, 44, 65
al-Muzarrid ibn Ḍirār: life of, 93; qasida of, xxxii, 29–33, 93–94, 95, 97

nabʿ, 68
al-Nāshi' al-Akbar, 99
Nawār, 24, 26
necklaces, 4, 25
nonhumans: distinctions between humans and, xxvi–xxvii; hunted, xxix–xxx; hunters, xxvii–xxviii. *See also under specific nonhumans*
north wind, 10, 23–28, 59, 91
Nubāyiʿ (wadi), 35

oceans, 5, 12
ochre, 42
oil, 7, 10, 20, 31, 32
onagers: compared to camels, 10, 91, 103, 106; in epistle, 76; hardship and success of, 91–92; killing of, xix, xxv, 72–73, 95, 98; in poems' texts, 5, 10, 12, 24, 30, 35, 39, 71, 72, 73; mention of, xix, xxv, xxx, xl, 91, 92, 95, 98, 103, 105, 106, 107
onyx, 6
orators, 32
Orion, 35, 56, 96
orphans, 15, 20, 28, 88
oryxes: compared to camels, 24, 59, 91; giving battle, 63–64; hardship and success of, 91–92; killing of, xix, 36, 64, 81, 95; in poems' texts, 6, 10, 23, 24, 29, 36, 59, 63–64; mention of, xix, xxv, xxx, 81, 89, 91–92, 95, 103, 105
ostriches, xv, xvii, xix, xx, xxxiv, 5, 6, 18, 23, 27, 54, 56, 70, 72, 102–103, 105
Oswald, Alice, xv–xxi, 96
outlaw poets (*ṣaʿālīk*), 87, 90

palaces, 61, 65
papyrus, 29
parataxis, xli, 79
partridges, xxx
pearls, xli, 12, 25, 59, 75, 84
pellet bows, xl
peppercorns, 3, 7
perches, 43, 48, 63
peregrine falcons (*shāhīn*), xxviii, xxix–xxx, xxxiii, 76, 107. *See also* falcons; saker falcons
perfumes, 6, 65
plants, 63, 66, 71, 75, 109. *See also under names of plants, shrubs, and herbs*
Pleiades, 4, 96
plunder, 9, 28
poems: in poems' texts, 12, 32; selection for this book, xxxix–xl. *See also under names of specific poems*
poetry: Anglo-Saxon, 84, 94; formal features of, xl–xli, 99; hegemony of the line in, xviii, xli; humans/nonhumans in, xxvi–xxx; in poems' texts, 12–13, 32; relationality in, xxvi–xxvii, 89; stress patterns in, xlii; translating of, xli–xlii; Welsh, 94. *See also* hunting complex; meters; *ṭardiyyah*

poets, xvii, xxiii–xxx, xxxii–xxxiii, xxxvi, xxxix, 12, 33, 79, 80, 83, 85, 87, 93. *See also under names of specific poets*
ponds, xxix, 19, 25, 29, 35, 46, 76
pots, 7, 69, 70, 72, 106
poverty, 19, 26, 31, 33, 38, 57, 88, 97
prose epistles. *See under* ʿAbd al-Ḥamīd al-Kātib
psalters, 23

Qafā Ḥibirr (mountains), 8
Qahr (hills), 24
Qalīb, 8
Qanān (mountains), 7
Qaṭan (mountains), 7
quarries, xxv, xxvii, xxix–xxxii, xl, 6, 17, 40, 43, 64, 74–76, 98
quivers, 35, 39, 68, 72
qullām (plant), 25
Quryān, 71
Quṣwān, 60
Quṭabiyyāt (mountain or water hole), 8

rags, 22, 27
raids/raiding/raiders, xxiv, 9, 15, 16, 17, 19, 27, 31, 35, 64, 76, 80, 84, 85, 88
rains, xix, xxv, 12, 19, 21, 23, 24, 25, 26, 28, 29, 36, 40, 53, 59, 66, 71, 75, 81, 84, 102
rajaz meter, xxxiii, xlii, 102, 104, 107
Rākis, 8
Rammān (mountains), 29
raptors. *See under specific raptors*
raqam, 33
ravines, xxix, 18
Rayyān (mountains), 23
relationality, xxvi–xxvii, 89
Rijām (mountains), 23
rocks, 5, 7, 11, 13, 18, 21, 23, 24, 30, 31, 40, 47, 54, 55, 61, 69, 89
roses, 54
royal hunts, xxxi–xxxii, 81, 90
ruins, 3, 14, 23, 85
Rukhām (mountains), 24

ṣaʿālīk (outlaw poets). *See* outlaw poets
saddles, 3, 4, 7, 17, 27, 36, 56, 60, 61, 62
Sadīr, 69
safflower, 71
saffron, 15, 42, 44, 60, 86
Ṣāʿidī, 35
saker falcons (*ṣaqr*), xxvii, xxviii, xxix, xxx, xxxiii, 15, 31, 76, 107. *See also* falcons; peregrine falcons
salaʿ (plant), 55
Salmā, 29, 93
salukis, xxiii, xxviii, xxx, 33, 103
Samāwah (desert), 61
Samharī, 26
sand dunes, 32
sandals, 19
sandgrouse, 19, 27, 61, 88, 89. *See also* grouse
sandworms, 5
ṣaqr (saker falcon). *See* saker falcons (*ṣaqr*)
sarīʿ meter, 85–86
Ṣarīḥ, 30–31
Sawāʾ, 35
scars, 10, 71
scarves, 20
*See*ling, 99
Seidensticker, Tilman, xlivn14, 102
sentries, 4, 24
Shābah (mountains), 14

shāhīn (peregrine falcon). *See* peregrine falcons
al-Shamardal ibn Sharīk: life of, 100–101; qasidas of, 43–52, 100–102
shame, 15, 18, 27, 28, 39, 88
al-Shammākh ibn Ḍirār, 93
al-Shanfarā: life of, 86–87; qasida of, xl, 17–20, 86–89
Shaybān, xxxvii, 56, 102
sheepdogs, 68
shields, 13, 20, 31
shīḥ (shrub), 53
shihrī, 75
al-Shimshāṭī, ʿAlī ibn Muḥammad, 99–100, 104
shrines, 6, 34, 96
Shurayf, 15
al-Shwēʿir, Ḥmēdān, 84
silk, 3, 24, 66
simʿ, 19
Simms, Colin, xi, 96
Sitār (hills), 7
skewers, 36, 44
slaves, 35
Smith, Rex, xxxiii, xlivn14, xlivn15
smiths, 32, 35
smoke, 15, 25
snakes. *See* vipers
souls, 8, 16, 18, 26, 33, 34, 60, 68, 69, 88, 92
south wind, 33, 24
sparrow hawks, xxxiii
sparrows, 61
spears, 26, 28, 31, 32, 35, 37, 41, 56, 76, 93
spindles, 7
spoils, 9, 17, 28, 43
spring, 23, 28, 59
springing, xxiii, 21
springs, 8, 29, 67
stars, xx, xxv, 5, 12, 21, 23, 25, 28, 40, 56, 59, 66, 80
storms, 7, 23, 53, 79, 80, 81, 83, 84, 102, 105
streams, 5, 8
stress patterns, xlii
Ṣuʿāʾid (wadi), 25
Ṣubāḥī, 33, 94
subsistence hunting, xxiii, xxxi–xxxii, 90
al-Sukkarī, Abū Saʿīd al-Ḥasan, 96
al-Ṣūlī, Muḥammad ibn Yaḥyā, 101
summer, xxv, 21, 106
sun, 19, 27, 31, 43, 46, 54, 59, 61, 65, 71, 72, 75
Ṣunaybiʿāt (water hole), 64
"The Suspended Odes" (*Muʿallaqāt*). *See Muʿallaqāt*
suṭṭāḥ (plant), 55
Ṣuwāʾiq, 24
sword belts, 3, 57
swords, 3, 32, 57, 62, 88, 93

Tabālah (wadi), xxxvii, 27
Taghlam (water hole), 14
ṭaḥmāʾ (shrub), 53
talons, 11, 41, 42, 43, 46, 75, 76
tamarisks, xx, 24
Tamīm, xxxvii, 69, 100, 105
Ṭams, xvi, 46
Ṭarafah ibn al-ʿAbd, 85
ṭardiyyah (pl. *ṭardiyyāt*): cheetahs in, xxviii; complete hunting scenes in, 81; as genre, xvi–xx, xxiii–xxxvi, xxxix–xl, 81, 83, 89, 98–99, 100, 101, 107; nonhumans in, xxiv–xxx, xxxv–xxxvi, xliiin7; quarries in, xxix–xxx; salukis in, xxviii. *See also* hunting complex; poetry

ṭarfāʾ (tamarisk), 54
tattoos, 23
Taymāʾ, 7
Tazīdī (garment), 35
teals (*burkah*), xxix
tears, xv, 3, 4, 8, 14, 34, 80
temples, 6
Tennyson, Alfred, xlii, 82
tents, xx, 4, 6, 15, 27, 30, 31, 55, 58, 64
terminal monorhyme, xl–xli
Thabīr (mountains), 7
thaghāmah (plant), 29
Thalabūt (wadi), 24
threnodies (*marthiyah*s). *See marthiyah*s
Thuʿālibāt, 8
thunder, 23, 59
al-Tibrīzī, Yaḥyā ibn ʿAlī, 83
timbrels, 30
time, xvii–xviii, xxv–xxvi, xxvii, 34, 53
tooth sticks, 5, 70
torrents, 6, 23, 81, 102
translating, of poetry, xv, xviii–xix, xxvii, xl–xlii
trebuchets, 47
trees, 5, 7, 14, 15, 25, 27, 38, 40, 54, 58, 59, 60, 66, 75, 76
tribal boasts (*fakhr*). *See fakhr*
trompo, 6
troughs, 53, 54, 105
truffles, 54
trumpets, 76
Tubbaʿ, 31, 37
Tūḍiḥ, 3, 24
Ṭulkhām (wadi), 24
turbans, xviii, 21, 57
Twin Mountains, 24
ʿUdhayb (water hole), 7
Uḥāẓah, 19
ʿUmar ibn al-Khaṭṭāb, caliph, 97
Umaymah, 34
Umm al-ʿAmr, 65
Umm Ḥuwayrith, 3
Umm Rabāb, 3
ʿUnayzah, 3, 80
ʿUthmān, caliph, 93, 95

veils, 24
vellum, 14
vengeance, xl, 62, 80, 81, 86, 87, 88–89, 92
vipers, 15, 17, 20, 21, 63, 67, 72, 88, 98, 105, 106
virgins, 6
vultures, 15

wadis, xxix, xxxvii, 5, 8, 23, 25, 59, 61, 72, 76. *See also under names of specific wadis*
Wagner, Ewald, xlivn14
Wajrah (steppe), 4, 24
warhorses. *See* horses
wars, 9, 14, 15, 19, 23, 28, 29, 30, 58, 80, 87, 93, 100, 108. *See also* battles/battlefields
water, xvii, xix, xx, 5, 7, 8, 12, 19, 20, 23, 25, 27, 31, 33, 35, 39, 53, 54, 58, 67, 70, 71, 72, 76, 81, 88, 92, 95, 102, 105, 106. *See also* oceans; ponds; springs; streams; torrents; water holes; wells
water carriers, xix, xx, 54. *See also* waterskins
water holes, xxix, xl, 53, 61, 71, 92, 95, 102. *See also under names of specific water holes*

waterskins, 5, 53. *See also* water carriers
weapons. *See* arrows; bows; knives; lances; spears; swords
Weipert, Reinhart, xxix, xxx
wells, xv, xx, 19, 33, 54, 69
Welsh poetry, 94
White, T. H., xxxv
Whitman, Walt, 83
widows/widowhood, 20, 28, 88
Williams, Rowan, 94
winds, xix, xxxiv, 3, 10, 18, 20, 22, 24, 25, 26, 28, 36, 45, 50, 54, 59, 66, 75. *See also* east wind; north wind; south wind
wines, 7, 26, 70
winter, xxv, 21
wolves, xv, xxxiv, 5, 6, 7, 17, 18, 20, 25, 26, 30, 35, 33, 45, 62, 80, 88, 89, 92, 101, 102

Yabrīn (desert), xxxvii, 61
Yadhbul (mountains), 5, 7
yarak, 31, 42
Yazan, 37

ẓabys, xxix, 6,
Zayed bin Sultan Al Nahyan, xxxiv, xlivn15
al-Zayn, Aḥmad, 96

About the NYU Abu Dhabi Research Institute

The Library of Arabic Literature is a research center affiliated with NYU Abu Dhabi and is supported by a grant from the NYU Abu Dhabi Research Institute.

The NYU Abu Dhabi Research Institute is a world-class center of cutting-edge and innovative research, scholarship, and cultural activity. It supports centers that address questions of global significance and local relevance and allows leading faculty members from across the disciplines to carry out creative scholarship and high-level research on a range of complex issues with depth, scale, and longevity that otherwise would not be possible.

From genomics and climate science to the humanities and Arabic literature, Research Institute centers make significant contributions to scholarship, scientific understanding, and artistic creativity. Centers strengthen cross-disciplinary engagement and innovation among the faculty, build critical mass in infrastructure and research talent at NYU Abu Dhabi, and have helped make the university a magnet for outstanding faculty, scholars, students, and international collaborations.

About the Translator

James E. Montgomery is Sir Thomas Adams's Professor of Arabic, Fellow of Trinity Hall at the University of Cambridge, and an Executive Editor of the Library of Arabic Literature. In 2024 he was elected Fellow of the British Academy.

The Library of Arabic Literature

For more details on individual titles, visit www.libraryofarabicliterature.org

Classical Arabic Literature: A Library of Arabic Literature Anthology
Selected and translated by Geert Jan van Gelder (2012)

A Treasury of Virtues: Sayings, Sermons, and Teachings of ʿAlī, by al-Qāḍī al-Quḍāʿī, with the *One Hundred Proverbs* attributed to al-Jāḥiẓ
Edited and translated by Tahera Qutbuddin (2013)

The Epistle on Legal Theory, by al-Shāfiʿī
Edited and translated by Joseph E. Lowry (2013)

Leg over Leg, by Aḥmad Fāris al-Shidyāq
Edited and translated by Humphrey Davies (4 volumes; 2013–14)

Virtues of the Imām Aḥmad ibn Ḥanbal, by Ibn al-Jawzī
Edited and translated by Michael Cooperson (2 volumes; 2013–15)

The Epistle of Forgiveness, by Abū l-ʿAlāʾ al-Maʿarrī
Edited and translated by Geert Jan van Gelder and Gregor Schoeler (2 volumes; 2013–14)

The Principles of Sufism, by ʿĀʾishah al-Bāʿūniyyah
Edited and translated by Th. Emil Homerin (2014)

The Expeditions: An Early Biography of Muḥammad, by Maʿmar ibn Rāshid
Edited and translated by Sean W. Anthony (2014)

Two Arabic Travel Books

Accounts of China and India, by Abū Zayd al-Sīrāfī
Edited and translated by Tim Mackintosh-Smith (2014)

Mission to the Volga, by Aḥmad ibn Faḍlān
Edited and translated by James Montgomery (2014)

Disagreements of the Jurists: A Manual of Islamic Legal Theory, by al-Qāḍī al-Nuʿmān
Edited and translated by Devin J. Stewart (2015)

Consorts of the Caliphs: Women and the Court of Baghdad, by Ibn al-Sāʿī
Edited by Shawkat M. Toorawa and translated by the Editors of the Library of Arabic Literature (2015)

What ʿĪsā ibn Hishām Told Us, by Muḥammad al-Muwayliḥī
Edited and translated by Roger Allen (2 volumes; 2015)

The Life and Times of Abū Tammām, by Abū Bakr Muḥammad ibn Yaḥyā al-Ṣūlī
Edited and translated by Beatrice Gruendler (2015)

The Sword of Ambition: Bureaucratic Rivalry in Medieval Egypt, by ʿUthmān ibn Ibrāhīm al-Nābulusī
Edited and translated by Luke Yarbrough (2016)

Brains Confounded by the Ode of Abū Shādūf Expounded, by Yūsuf al-Shirbīnī
Edited and translated by Humphrey Davies (2 volumes; 2016)

Light in the Heavens: Sayings of the Prophet Muḥammad, by al-Qāḍī al-Quḍāʿī
Edited and translated by Tahera Qutbuddin (2016)

Risible Rhymes, by Muḥammad ibn Maḥfūẓ al-Sanhūrī
Edited and translated by Humphrey Davies (2016)

A Hundred and One Nights
Edited and translated by Bruce Fudge (2016)

The Excellence of the Arabs, by Ibn Qutaybah
Edited by James E. Montgomery and Peter Webb
Translated by Sarah Bowen Savant and Peter Webb (2017)

Scents and Flavors: A Syrian Cookbook
Edited and translated by Charles Perry (2017)

Arabian Satire: Poetry from 18th-Century Najd, by Ḥmēdān al-Shwēʿir
Edited and translated by Marcel Kurpershoek (2017)

In Darfur: An Account of the Sultanate and Its People, by Muḥammad ibn ʿUmar al-Tūnisī
Edited and translated by Humphrey Davies (2 volumes; 2018)

War Songs, by ʿAntarah ibn Shaddād
Edited by James E. Montgomery
Translated by James E. Montgomery with Richard Sieburth (2018)

Arabian Romantic: Poems on Bedouin Life and Love, by ʿAbdallah ibn Sbayyil
Edited and translated by Marcel Kurpershoek (2018)

Dīwān ʿAntarah ibn Shaddād: A Literary-Historical Study, by James E. Montgomery (2018)

Stories of Piety and Prayer: Deliverance Follows Adversity, by al-Muḥassin ibn ʿAlī al-Tanūkhī
Edited and translated by Julia Bray (2019)

Tajrīd sayf al-himmah li-stikhrāj mā fī dhimmat al-dhimmah: A Scholarly Edition of ʿUthmān ibn Ibrāhīm al-Nābulusī's Text, by Luke Yarbrough (2019)

The Philosopher Responds: An Intellectual Correspondence from the Tenth Century, by Abū Ḥayyān al-Tawḥīdī and Abū ʿAlī Miskawayh
Edited by Bilal Orfali and Maurice A. Pomerantz
Translated by Sophia Vasalou and James E. Montgomery (2 volumes; 2019)

The Discourses: Reflections on History, Sufism, Theology, and Literature—Volume One, by al-Ḥasan al-Yūsī
Edited and translated by Justin Stearns (2020)

Impostures, by al-Ḥarīrī
Translated by Michael Cooperson (2020)

Maqāmāt Abī Zayd al-Sarūjī, by al-Ḥarīrī
Edited by Michael Cooperson (2020)

The Yoga Sutras of Patañjali, by Abū Rayḥān al-Bīrūnī
Edited and translated by Mario Kozah (2020)

The Book of Charlatans, by Jamāl al-Dīn ʿAbd al-Raḥīm al-Jawbarī
Edited by Manuela Dengler
Translated by Humphrey Davies (2020)

A Physician on the Nile: A Description of Egypt and Journal of the Famine Years, by ʿAbd al-Laṭīf al-Baghdādī
Edited and translated by Tim Mackintosh-Smith (2021)

The Book of Travels, by Ḥannā Diyāb
Edited by Johannes Stephan
Translated by Elias Muhanna (2 volumes; 2021)

Kalīlah and Dimnah: Fables of Virtue and Vice, by Ibn al-Muqaffaʿ
Edited by Michael Fishbein
Translated by Michael Fishbein and James E. Montgomery (2021)

Love, Death, Fame: Poetry and Lore from the Emirati Oral Tradition, by al-Māyidī ibn Ẓāhir
Edited and translated by Marcel Kurpershoek (2022)

The Essence of Reality: A Defense of Philosophical Sufism, by ʿAyn al-Quḍāt
Edited and translated by Mohammed Rustom (2022)

The Requirements of the Sufi Path: A Defense of the Mystical Tradition, by Ibn Khaldūn
Edited and translated by Carolyn Baugh (2022)

The Doctors' Dinner Party, by Ibn Buṭlān
Edited and translated by Philip F. Kennedy and Jeremy Farrell (2023)

Fate the Hunter: Early Arabic Hunting Poems
Edited and translated by James E. Montgomery (2023)

The Book of Monasteries, by al-Shābushtī
Edited and translated by Hilary Kilpatrick (2023)

In Deadly Embrace: Arabic Hunting Poems, by Ibn al-Muʿtazz
Edited and translated by James E. Montgomery (2023)

The Divine Names, by ʿAfīf al-Dīn al-Tilimsānī
Edited and translated by Yousef Casewit (2023)

Bedouin Poets of the Nafūd Desert, by Khalaf Abū Zwayyid, ʿAdwān al-Hirbīd, and ʿAjlān ibn Rmāl
Edited and translated by Marcel Kurpershoek (2024)

The Rules of Logic, by Najm al-Dīn al-Kātibī
Edited and translated by Tony Street (2024)

Najm al-dīn al-Kātibī's al-Risālah al-Shamsiyyah: An Edition and Translation with Commentary, by Tony Street (2024)

A Demon Spirit: Arabic Hunting Poems, by Abū Nuwās
Edited and translated by James E. Montgomery (2024)

Arabian Hero: Oral Poetry and Narrative Lore from Northern Arabia, by Shāyiʿ al-Amsaḥ
Edited and translated by Marcel Kurpershoek (2024)

English-only Paperbacks

Leg over Leg, by Aḥmad Fāris al-Shidyāq (2 volumes; 2015)

The Expeditions: An Early Biography of Muḥammad, by Maʿmar ibn Rāshid (2015)

The Epistle on Legal Theory: A Translation of al-Shāfiʿī's Risālah, by al-Shāfiʿī (2015)

The Epistle of Forgiveness, by Abū l-ʿAlāʾ al-Maʿarrī (2016)

The Principles of Sufism, by ʿĀʾishah al-Bāʿūniyyah (2016)

A Treasury of Virtues: Sayings, Sermons, and Teachings of ʿAlī, by al-Qāḍī al-Quḍāʿī with the *One Hundred Proverbs* attributed to al-Jāḥiẓ (2016)

The Life of Ibn Ḥanbal, by Ibn al-Jawzī (2016)

Mission to the Volga, by Ibn Faḍlān (2017)

Accounts of China and India, by Abū Zayd al-Sīrāfī (2017)

Consorts of the Caliphs: Women and the Court of Baghdad, by Ibn al-Sāʿī (2017)

A Hundred and One Nights (2017)

Disagreements of the Jurists: A Manual of Islamic Legal Theory, by al-Qāḍī al-Nuʿmān (2017)

What ʿĪsā ibn Hishām Told Us, by Muḥammad al-Muwayliḥī (2018)

War Songs, by ʿAntarah ibn Shaddād (2018)

The Life and Times of Abū Tammām, by Abū Bakr Muḥammad ibn Yaḥyā al-Ṣūlī (2018)

The Sword of Ambition, by ʿUthmān ibn Ibrāhīm al-Nābulusī (2019)

Brains Confounded by the Ode of Abū Shādūf Expounded: Volume One, by Yūsuf al-Shirbīnī (2019)

Brains Confounded by the Ode of Abū Shādūf Expounded: Volume Two, by Yūsuf al-Shirbīnī and *Risible Rhymes*, by Muḥammad ibn Maḥfūẓ al-Sanhūrī (2019)

The Excellence of the Arabs, by Ibn Qutaybah (2019)

Light in the Heavens: Sayings of the Prophet Muḥammad, by al-Qāḍī al-Quḍāʿī (2019)

Scents and Flavors: A Syrian Cookbook (2020)

Arabian Satire: Poetry from 18th-Century Najd, by Ḥmēdān al-Shwēʿir (2020)

In Darfur: An Account of the Sultanate and Its People, by Muḥammad al-Tūnisī (2020)

Arabian Romantic: Poems on Bedouin Life and Love, by Ibn Sbayyil (2020)

The Philosopher Responds: An Intellectual Correspondence from the Tenth Century, by Abū Ḥayyān al-Tawḥīdī and Abū ʿAlī Miskawayh (2021)

Impostures, by al-Ḥarīrī (2021)

The Discourses: Reflections on History, Sufism, Theology, and Literature—Volume One, by al-Ḥasan al-Yūsī (2021)

The Yoga Sutras of Patañjali, by Abū Rayḥān al-Bīrūnī (2022)

The Book of Charlatans, by Jamāl al-Dīn ʿAbd al-Raḥīm al-Jawbarī (2022)

The Book of Travels, by Ḥannā Diyāb (2022)

A Physician on the Nile: A Description of Egypt and Journal of the Famine Years, by ʿAbd al-Laṭīf al-Baghdādī (2022)

Kalīlah and Dimnah: Fables of Virtue and Vice, by Ibn al-Muqaffaʿ (2023)

Love, Death, Fame: Poetry and Lore from the Emirati Oral Tradition, by al-Māyidī ibn Ẓāhir (2023)

The Essence of Reality: A Defense of Philosophical Sufism, by ʿAyn al-Quḍāt (2023)

The Doctors' Dinner Party, by Ibn Buṭlān (2024)

The Requirements of the Sufi Path: A Defense of the Mystical Tradition, by Ibn Khaldūn (2024)

Fate the Hunter: Early Arabic Hunting Poems (2024)

www.ingramcontent.com/pod-product-compliance
Lightning Source LLC
Chambersburg PA
CBHW020412080526
44584CB00014B/1290
9781479834259